The REAL Longevity Authority

95-Year-Old Twins' Advice for a Happy, Healthy Life

EVITA & LIONEL LONGE

MINERVA DOY
PUBLISHING

Paperback ISBN: 978-1-7646319-3-8

Hardcover ISBN: 978-1-7646319-4-5

Ebook ISBN: 978-1-7646319-5-2

For Blythe, UK, and Old Trousers, with love

And for those still curious, still kind, still here

About the Authors

Evita and Lionel Longe

- Nonagenarians

- Twins (we identify as non-identical)

- Life-long learners

- Quiet rebels against anti-ageing nonsense

- We've had interesting lives, but we won't bore you with the details

THE REAL LONGEVITY AUTHORITY

95-Year-Old Twins' Advice for a Happy, Healthy Life

Contents

Foreword

In a world full of self-proclaimed longevity experts who haven't even reached retirement age, here come two voices that have lived - and are living - the long journey. Every ache, every joy, every lesson.

Now in their mid-nineties, with a combined 190 years between them, twins Evita and Lionel Longe have outlasted diets, fitness crazes, and health fads — not through miracle supplements or biohacks, but through common sense, curiosity, and a generous dose of humor.

Through wars, technological revolutions, and personal challenges, they've discovered that longevity isn't just about surviving - it's about engaging fully with life at every age.

In The Real Longevity Authority, they share their life stories, their habits, mindsets, and quiet disciplines that help them live independently and happily into their tenth decade.

Part memoir, part manual, this is not a book about defying age — it's about inhabiting it fully. Grounded, candid, and uplifting, it's proof that the best longevity advice comes from those who have truly walked the distance.

Introduction

"Old age comes suddenly, and not gradually as is thought."

- Emily Dickinson

We never meant to become experts on ageing. We both simply kept waking up.

That, we suspect, is where most longevity journeys begin — not with supplements or ice baths, but with the small, stubborn act of staying alive and paying attention.

When people find out our age, they're often taken aback, assuming we're in our seventies or early eighties.

Once they've recovered, the next question is usually, "What's your secret?"

We always smile, because they expect deep wisdom or a bizarre formula — kale, yoga, meditation, perhaps a miracle supplement.

Sometimes - because we're cheeky - we are tempted to make up a fake anti-aging solution, like standing on our heads for two hours a day. Just to see if they'd consider it.

But the truth is simpler, and perhaps not as gratifying for our audience: We've just been living.

You see, we've lived long enough to see the world reinvent 'wellness' at least a dozen times.

We've listened to all the modern longevity 'experts' talk about telomeres, mitochondria, and micro-something-or-other. They sound impressive, but few of them have actually made it past ninety.

We have — and let us tell you, the real secrets are less scientific and far more amusing.

Every decade brings a new secret to living longer: cold plunges, collagen, and now something called 'biohacking.'

We've lived long enough to see fads come and go — the grapefruit diet, the low-fat craze, and the era of bottled oxygen. The only thing that's truly endured is the human need for connection, movement, laughter, and a good meal shared with someone who listens.

We don't know about you, but we've never once seen a ninety-year-old who credits their good health to an app, a smartwatch, or powdered mushrooms.

What we have seen - and lived - are the quieter, steadier things that keep a person going. A daily walk. A good laugh. Food cooked at home, often shared. A reason to get out of bed, even on the mornings when your knees argue otherwise.

We're ninety-five now - old enough to have watched friends, siblings, and even doctors come and go. We're old enough to know that longevity is not about avoiding age, but inhabiting it fully.

When we look back, we see that we didn't plan to live this long. We simply lived well enough each day - and the years added up. We walked instead of worrying about our step count. We ate vegetables because we grew them. We laughed because it felt better than complaining.

The irony is that we're now considered "longevity authorities" by default - not because we studied it, but because we've both survived the lot. We don't have PhDs, but we do have 190 years between us of personally tested experience, under all sorts of conditions.

In The Real Longevity Authority, we share the habits, mindsets, and quiet disciplines that have helped us live independently and happily into our tenth decade. Blending memoir and practical wisdom, we offer detailed reflections on how to keep your body moving (even when it protests), the daily habits that matter most, food and sleep rhythms, the importance of purpose and gratitude, and how to make peace with change and loss.

This book isn't about chasing youth - it's about staying upright, curious, and grateful as the decades unfold. It's a guide to the simple habits that work - and a few of the ones that don't. It's also a story about the grace that comes with time: how to make peace with the body that changes, the people you lose, and the world that keeps spinning faster than you can keep up.

We're not against science or new ideas. We just believe that the real science of longevity is written in the human face - the lines, the smiles, the eyes that still light up when life surprises them.

This book isn't written by a scientist or longevity gurus. It's written by two people who have had the great privilege of time and who remain ongoing, living testaments to what actually works.

This book isn't a manual; it's a conversation. A mix of memoir and guide, of stories and small rules we've experienced first-hand or collected while outliving most of the experts. You'll find no promises of immortality here — just a few truths about how to live long enough to be glad you did.

This book is for everyone still learning how to grow old without growing dull —and for those wise enough to start early.

We don't promise you more years. But we can promise this: the ones you have will feel fuller, lighter, and more truly yours.

So let's start there - with the ordinary, everyday things that truly matter.

Because longevity isn't a number. It's a way of being.

We hope you'll read these pages the way we wrote them: with a cup of tea in hand, a sense of humour intact, and no rush whatsoever.

Because if there's one lesson longevity has taught us both, it's this: The slower you go, the more of life you actually meet.

So — take your time. We certainly have.

Evita and Lionel

Chapter I

Twin Perspectives

The Myths of Longevity Gurus

I'm not young enough to know everything.

- Oscar Wilde

We, fraternal (non-identical) twins, Evita and Lionel, were born during the Depression, at a time when one extra mouth to feed was difficult, let alone two.

Our mother, despite being much larger in this, her second, pregnancy, expected one baby and never really recovered from the shock of two teeny ones, a girl and a boy, born seven weeks early.

There were no ultrasounds or IVF back then, and multiple births were uncommon. Our father had recently found work in his trade as a cooper, or barrel-maker, so considered our arrival a good omen.

Lionel's little head was no bigger than a fine china teacup, and just as fragile. Being so small and weak, he was hastily Christened and set aside, not expected to live.

Over nine decades later, the joke's on the poor medical staff of the time, long since departed.

As we write, Lionel has just had his driver's licence renewed and often drives to visit his niece, two hours away.

Evita, recently widowed, lives quietly but independently. Her senses of style and humour ensure she's always surrounded by much younger friends; she having outlived most of her old ones.

Having 'good' genes helps, but our parents were not what we would now consider 'SuperAgers'.

Our mother died at 66 from breast cancer. In spite of huge medical advances made by the mid-20th Century, preventative medicine was not what it is today. A cancer diagnosis was often made too late for intervention and spelled certain death. Poor Mum gave up and spent her final months only interested in eating packet biscuits.

Our father, always with a sparkle in his eye, lived to 84. This was remarkable, as he'd smoked a pipe for all his adult life. We still remember his ritual of packing that infernal pipe, and us buying him packets of pipe cleaners - which, surprisingly, they're still known as - for Christmas. Who knows how much longer he may have lived, had his lungs not resembled old underpants elastic: dry, crackly and completely unyielding.

Apart from the usual teenage experimentation, neither of us has ever taken up smoking, the result of years of rainy Sunday drives with Dad puffing on his pipe, and the car windows up.

We're not big drinkers, either, although we could hardly be described as tee-totalers. We will have the occasional beer or glass of wine for the pleasure of it, rather than to get hammered. It's simply not worth feeling horrible, hungover and dehydrated the following day. We know we wouldn't recover from binges as well as we used to.

While we don't count calories, we've always kept our weight in check by refusing to go up a clothing size. If clothes start feeling uncomfortable, it's time to rein ourselves in.

So there is discipline involved. But it doesn't have to be strict when everything is done in moderation.

This may sound too good to be true, but remember this is a book about longevity and, to be brutally honest, we need to ask ourselves why there are very few obese, alcoholic, smoking nonagenarians around.

Reinventions of Wellness

The industry would have us believe that the secret to longevity lies in exotic supplements, complex biohacking routines, or expensive anti-aging treatments. But after living through nine decades and witnessing countless health fads come and go, we've learned that the truth about living long and well is far simpler - and far less expensive.

We don't know about you, but we've never once seen a ninety-year-old who credits their good health to an app, a smartwatch, or powdered mushrooms. Although Lionel has started drinking beetroot smoothies before bed. Good for the libido, he jokes, while Evita rolls her eyes.

What we have seen — and lived — are the quieter, steadier things that keep a person going. A daily walk. A good laugh. Food cooked at home, often shared. A reason to get out of bed, even on the mornings when your knees argue otherwise.

The Rise of Modern Longevity Marketing

The wellness industry has transformed dramatically during our lifetimes, morphing from simple folk wisdom into a complex commercial enterprise. We've watched as traditional advice about eating well and staying active has been overshadowed by sophisticated marketing campaigns promising eternal youth through expensive supplements, devices, and programs.

Every few years, a new wave of self-proclaimed longevity experts emerges, armed with scientific terminology and promises of revolutionary breakthroughs. They speak of biohacking, cellular rejuvenation, and anti-aging protocols - often without having lived long enough to test their own theories. We find ourselves chuckling at thirty-something wellness divas confidently explaining how to reach eighty while we've quietly done more than that, without their expensive interventions.

The modern longevity market has become increasingly sophisticated in its approach. Social media platforms are flooded with influencers promoting everything from ice baths to mushroom gummies, each claiming to hold the key to extended youth. These new authorities often present their advice with scientific precision, though their evidence is frequently preliminary or anecdotal.

We've observed how this commercialization of wellness has created what we call 'expert anxiety' - people becoming so overwhelmed by conflicting advice that they lose touch with their own body's wisdom. They track every step, measure every morsel, and worry about every wrinkle, often forgetting to actually enjoy their lives in the process.

In contrast, our contemporaries who've reached their nineties tend to share remarkably similar stories - ones of simple living, consistent habits, and measured indulgence.

Take the famous example of Britain's beloved Tipton twins, Lilian Cox and Doris Hobday, who famously credited their longevity to "No sex and plenty of Guinness" – slightly more credible than Lionel hanging upside down daily. Hardly the kind of advice you'd find in a modern wellness blog, but they thrived well into their nineties with this approach. They maintained active social lives, enjoyed their favorite foods without guilt, and emphasized laughter over restriction.

The truth about longevity marketing is that it often overcomplicates what should be straightforward. While science has certainly advanced our understanding of aging, the basic principles of living well haven't changed as dramatically as marketing would have us believe. The body's fundamental needs remain remarkably consistent: movement, nourishment, rest, purpose, and connection.

We've watched countless 'miracle' products come and go - each promising to be the key to extended life. Yet here we are, having outlived many of these trends, simply by sticking to the basics: eating real food, staying active, maintaining social connections, and finding joy in ordinary days.

Perhaps the most ironic aspect of modern longevity marketing is how it often creates stress about aging - the very thing that can accelerate the aging process. We've seen people become so anxious about optimizing their health that they forget to actually live their lives.

The modern wellness industry would have you believe that living a long, healthy life requires elaborate protocols, expensive supplements, and constant monitoring. But our experience, like that of many nonagenarians, tells a different story. The truth about longevity isn't found in a bottle or a biohacking device - it's written in the simple patterns of daily life.

Common Sense vs Commercial Promises

The people who live longest, in our observation, aren't chasing eternal youth or health; they're living it. They get up, move their bodies, eat simple food, stay social, and keep their curiosity alive. They don't set themselves unrealistic goals nor punish themselves with impossible rules. They know that discipline without joy turns sour.

Longevity isn't an extreme sport. It's quiet consistency — the gentle rhythm of ordinary days done well. The body thrives on routine, moderation, and kindness. We've just made those ideas too dull to market.

The contrast between common sense and commercial promises in longevity becomes stark when you've lived long enough to see countless wellness trends come and go. We've watched as simple truths about health have been repackaged and marketed back to us in increasingly complex and expensive forms.

Our advice? Take what serves you from modern wellness wisdom, but don't let it overshadow the simple truths that have stood the test of time. After all, the best evidence for what works isn't found in a laboratory or on a social media feed - it's found in the lives of those who've actually achieved longevity through decades of real-world experience.

The Danger of Expert Anxiety

The problem with commercial promises is that they often create more stress than they solve. We've met people so worried about optimizing their longevity that they've forgotten to actually live. They track every step, measure every morsel, and worry about every wrinkle, while missing the simple pleasures that make life worth extending.

Anxiety ages you faster than the years - or chocolate - ever could.

Common sense tells us that the body knows what it needs - if we're willing to listen. It asks for movement, not necessarily marathon training. It wants real food, not processed supplements. It thrives on connection, not isolation in pursuit of perfect health.

We're not against progress or scientific advancement. But we've noticed that the most effective health practices tend to be the simplest ones - the kinds that don't require a manual or a subscription. Walking daily. Eating meals with friends. Getting enough sleep. Laughing often. These aren't secrets - they're just truths that have stood the test of time.

The irony of modern longevity marketing is how it often complicates what should be straightforward. While science has certainly advanced our understanding of aging, the basic principles of living well haven't changed as dramatically as marketing would have us believe. The body's fundamental needs remain remarkably consistent: movement, nourishment, rest, purpose, and connection.

Perhaps the most telling evidence comes from our own experience and that of our long-lived peers. Those who've reached their nineties tend to share remarkably similar stories - ones of simple living, consistent habits, and measured indulgence. Not stories of rigorous biohacking or expensive anti-aging treatments.

Sustainable Habits That Actually Work

The most sustainable habits we've discovered aren't Instagram-worthy or expensive - they're the ones that feel natural enough to maintain for decades. Like Britain's Lilian Cox and Doris Hobday, we've found that the habits that actually work are often surprisingly simple and enjoyable.

First among these is the habit of moderation. Not strict dieting or intense exercise regimens, but a balanced approach to eating, drinking, and activity. We enjoy our meals without obsessing over every ingredient. We believe that pleasure has its place in a long life.

The second vital habit is maintaining social connections. The Tipton Twins lived next door to each other, supporting daily companionship and proving that regular social interaction is as important as any vitamin. We've seen countless studies and experts promote isolation in pursuit of health, but our experience shows that connection and community are essential for longevity.

Physical activity is crucial, but it doesn't need to be extreme. Like many who've taken up chair yoga and maintained their flexibility well into their 90s, we've found that gentle, consistent movement serves better than intense workout regimens. Walking, stretching, and staying active through daily tasks have kept us mobile without strain or injury.

Perhaps most importantly, we've maintained the habit of adaptability. With the help and encouragement of grandchildren, we've embraced social media. Keeping up with the world doesn't stop with age. We've seen too many peers become rigid in their ways, refusing to adapt to change. Those who live longest tend to be those who remain flexible - both in body and mind.

Another sustainable habit is maintaining independence while accepting help when needed. This balance keeps us active and engaged without risking our health through stubbornness. We've learned to modify activities rather than abandon them entirely, finding new ways to do what we love as our capabilities change.

Laughter and maintaining a sense of humor have been among our most cherished habits. The Tipton Twins were well known for their wit and playful banter, demonstrating how joy and laughter contribute to longevity. We've found that people who can laugh at life's challenges tend to weather them better.

Finally, we've maintained the habit of defining our own path to health. While some experts insist on specific routines or restrictions, we've learned to trust our experience and listen to our bodies. Like other oldies who have challenged or ignored conventional wisdom, we've found that personal autonomy in health choices often leads to better outcomes than following someone else's strict rules

Living Well: The Only Longevity Secret That Matters

These habits have sustained us not because they're revolutionary, but because they're realistic. They don't require expensive equipment or elaborate routines. They simply ask us to live mindfully, joyfully, and consistently. That's what makes them truly sustainable - they're habits that enhance life rather than restrict it.

When you've made it to ninety-five, you realise that lived experience is its own qualification. We've seen medicine advance, diets rise and fall, and exercise fads come and go. The constants are movement, moderation, purpose, and people.

We've outlasted every 'expert' we were encouraged to follow — not because we were smarter, but because we learned to listen to our own bodies. They tell you what they need, if you stop long enough to listen.

The Real Measure of Longevity

The true goal isn't to live longer; it's to live better. We don't count our years — we count how many of them we still enjoy.

So when the next shiny theory comes along promising to "reverse ageing," smile politely and go for a walk. The fresh air costs nothing, and it's worked for us every day so far.

As we conclude this first chapter, we're reminded that the pursuit of longevity isn't about following the latest trends or chasing miracle cures. It's about embracing the simple, sustainable practices that have stood the test of time.

We've shared our perspective on the modern wellness industry and its endless parade of experts, supplements, and quick fixes. But more importantly, we've introduced you to a different kind of wisdom - one earned through nine decades of actual living.

The truth about living long and well isn't found in expensive programs or complicated regimens. It's written in the quiet routines of those who've actually achieved it: daily walks, home-cooked meals, genuine connections, and the courage to laugh when life throws its inevitable curves.

We've watched countless health fads come and go. We've outlived many self-proclaimed experts. And what we've learned is this: longevity isn't something you can buy or hack - it's something you live, one mindful day at a time.

The chapters ahead will delve deeper into the practical aspects of living well: movement, nourishment, rest, purpose, and connection. But they all build on this fundamental truth: the best path to longevity is the one you can walk consistently, joyfully, and for the long haul.

We're not here to sell you a miracle or promise eternal youth. We're here to share what we've learned from actually living these years - all 190 of them between us. Because at the end of the day, the only longevity expert worth listening to is someone who's actually lived long enough to prove their theories.

So as we close this chapter, we invite you to set aside the complexity and embrace the simplicity. Stop chasing immortality and start living fully in each moment you're given. After all, that's not just the secret to living longer - it's the secret to living better.

In the next chapter, we'll explore how to keep your body moving without turning exercise into a chore. But for now, remember: the best longevity plan is one that makes you want to get up tomorrow and do it all again.

Our Rule for Longevity #1:

Ignore the fads and 'experts' and start doing what you can manage and enjoy.

This simple principle has carried us through ninety-five years, and it continues to serve us well.

CHAPTER 2

The Joy of Staying Active

MOVING DAILY WITHOUT OVERTHINKING

You know you're getting old when you bend down to tie your shoes and wonder what else you can do while you're down there.

– George Burns

When we were young, we didn't 'exercise' or work out for the sake of working out. We just did things. We walked to school - often barefoot, across paddocks filled with cowpats. We helped around the house, hung laundry, weeded gardens, carried groceries, and danced on weekends. Nobody called it cardio. It was simply life.

Now, we have so many choices available to us that it can be paralysing. HIIT or spin? Yoga or Pilates? Ten thousand steps, or just enough to post online? Some spend more time tracking their movement than actually moving.

We've never owned fitness bands or smartwatches. Our pulses don't need measuring - we can feel them when we climb the stairs. And if we can still reach the clothesline without wobbling, that's proof enough we're doing well.

Why Motion, Not Marathon, Keeps Us Young

The most valuable lesson we've learned about movement in our ninety-plus years isn't from a gym or a fitness guru - it's from watching the seasons change. Just as nature doesn't force growth but maintains a steady, gentle rhythm, our bodies thrive not on sporadic bursts of intense exercise, but on consistent, mindful movement throughout each day. Like everything else we've learned about movement and the body, this observation came not from a book or a guru, but from quietly watching the world around us. Just as nature doesn't strain or force, but moves with gentle persistence, our bodies thrive on steady, mindful motion rather than sporadic bursts of intense activity.

The Grace of Daily Motion

Movement is not punishment; it's a conversation with your body. Every day it asks: Will you use me today, or leave me to rust?

The human body wants to move - not for medals or marathons, just steady use. Those who stay strong into old age rarely try to outsmart biology. They simply keep going: gardening, walking, carrying their own bags, sometimes even dancing when no one's looking.

Lionel, when in his eighties, was often asked how he stayed so fit: I get up. And I keep getting up.

That's all it takes. The hardest part is beginning - every single day.

Life has taught us that movement doesn't need to be complicated to be effective. In fact, the simpler it is, the more likely we are to maintain it. Through nine decades of watching fads come and go, we've learned that the most sustainable exercise is the kind that fits naturally into your daily rhythm - the kind that becomes as automatic as breathing.

In this chapter, we'll explore how to make movement a natural, enjoyable part of your life. Not through complex routines or expensive equipment, but through simple, sustainable practices that have kept us mobile and independent.

Because at the end of the day, movement isn't about performance - it's about persistence. It's about finding ways to keep your body engaged and active that you can maintain not just for weeks or months, but for decades to come.

The Breath and the Mind

Breathing is the most overlooked exercise of all. Deep, steady breaths nourish every cell and calm every thought.

Evita: When I feel anxious — about health, loss, or the state of the world — I take five slow, deep breaths. It brings me back to where life is actually happening.

If you can stop, relax, and breathe deeply, you're already halfway to peace.

Start Where You Are

If you haven't moved in a while, start small. The body forgives, but it needs an invitation.

Stand more often. Stretch when you wake. Take short walks, adding a few steps each week. You're not competing with anyone — just reintroducing yourself to the body that's carried you this far.

Make Movement a Habit, Not an Event

You don't need a gym. You need routine. Walk when you can, stand when you'd normally sit, take the stairs when you can. Every small choice adds up.

Evita: I still hang washing outside, though I could use the dryer. It's not stubbornness — it's a small daily act that keeps me strong. And a little sun and air are better than any vitamin.

Lionel's neighbour Julia used to marvel at his mobility. She'd see him in the garden, squatting, bending, reaching.

"But when do you do your actual exercise?" she asked.

"This is my exercise," he said. "Natural movements, repeated daily."

Now in her eighties, Julia swears by Lionel's advice. "I've stopped counting steps," she says, "and started counting flowers instead."

Gentle Rules for Longevity Fitness

- **As soon as you wake, stretch before getting out of bed.**

- **Move every day, even ten mindful minutes.**

- **Stretch before you sit. Reach up before sinking into the chair.**

- **Balance is everything. Stand on one foot while brushing your teeth.**

- **Walk like you mean it. Shoulders back, chin up, eyes open.**

- **Rest with intention. Rest is not idleness — it's repair.**

The Pleasure of Walking and Natural Movement

The simple act of putting one foot in front of the other has carried us through nine decades of life. Walking isn't just exercise - it's a daily meditation, a gentle reminder that movement is life itself.

Evita: I've walked through joy and grief, through celebrations and losses. Each step has been both a physical act and a metaphor for living - steady, patient, forward-moving. Even now, my daily walks keep me connected not just to my body, but to the world around me.

Lionel: Walking has been my constant companion through life. No gym membership required, no special equipment needed - just a decent pair of shoes and the willingness to begin. Even on days when my joints protest, I know that movement is medicine.

The science supports what we've learned through experience. Research from Harvard Medical School confirms that walking 30 minutes daily reduces the risk of heart disease, stroke, diabetes, and several cancers. It improves mood and contributes to longevity. But we didn't need studies to tell us this - we've lived it.

We've watched countless exercise trends come and go - aerobics, spinning, high-intensity training. Meanwhile, walking remains the most natural, sustainable form of movement humans can do. It's what our bodies were designed for, and it's what keeps us moving well into our nineties.

The key is consistency, not intensity. A gentle daily walk does more for longevity than sporadic bursts of strenuous exercise. We've seen this truth played out in our own lives and in the lives of other nonagenarians we've known.

Natural movement goes beyond walking. It's about maintaining the basic motions that keep us independent - standing up from a chair, reaching for objects, bending to tie our shoes. These everyday movements, what scientists call 'functional fitness,' are the true foundation of a long, independent life.

The British Journal of Sports Medicine has found that even light-intensity, regular movement is associated with lower mortality risk in older adults. We're living proof of this research. Our independence at ninety-five comes not from any extreme exercise regimen, but from the simple habit of keeping our bodies in motion.

The Joy of Moving with Others

If you can, move in company. Walk with a friend, join a group, stroll through the markets. We forget we're exercising when we're talking.

Evita: When I lost my husband, it was walking with neighbours that saved me. I called it my grief club — not talking much about loss, but walking through it. Step by step, the world became bearable again.

We've learned to make movement social when possible. Walking with friends, stretching together, or simply moving through daily tasks in company - it all adds to the benefits. The Blue Zones Project, studying the world's longest-lived populations, consistently finds that natural, habitual movement combined with social connection is a shared trait among centenarians

Our advice is simple:

- **Walk daily, even if just for 10-15 minutes.**

- **Move naturally throughout the day.**

- **Make movement social when possible.**

- **Listen to your body's signals.**

- **Focus on consistency over intensity.**

Remember, it's not about breaking records or counting steps. It's about maintaining the natural movements that keep us independent and engaged with life. As we often say, the best exercise isn't the one that exhausts you - it's the one you'll still be doing in your nineties.

The human body is designed for movement, but it doesn't need to be complicated or strenuous. Simple, natural movement - walking, stretching, reaching, bending - these are the foundations of lasting mobility. We're still walking, still moving, still independent because we never stopped doing these basic things.

So, lace up or fasten your shoes, step outside, and remember - every walk is a celebration of life itself. Movement isn't just about adding years to your life; it's about adding life to your years.

The Power of Small, Consistent Effort

Lionel: In my seventies, I thought it was too late to start exercising. Then a physiotherapist said, 'It's never too late to build strength.' Within weeks of gentle walks and light weights, I noticed the difference — steadier steps, better sleep, clearer mind.

It's not about intensity; it's about consistency. The body rewards regular effort with quiet loyalty.

Building Movement into Daily Routines

The secret to staying active isn't found in expensive gym memberships or complicated workout routines - it's woven into the fabric of daily life. Through nine decades of experience, we've learned that the most sustainable movement is the kind that becomes as natural as breathing.

Evita: When I was younger, movement happened naturally through daily chores and activities. Now, I consciously build it into my routine. I stretch or squat while waiting for the kettle to boil. I do heel raises while brushing my teeth. These aren't exercises - they're just part of living.

Lionel: I've turned my daily tasks into opportunities for movement. Gardening becomes a full-body workout. Hanging my laundry becomes a stretching session. I walk to get my newspaper instead of having it delivered. This all keeps me moving in ways no gym could replicate.

America's Kaysville twins, Verla Starkey and Merla Swenson, have shared our philosophy. They maintained their vitality and flexibility through practical, everyday activities - from sewing to gardening to maintaining their households. These weren't exercises; they were just life tasks that kept them naturally active.

Here's what we've learned about building movement into daily life:

Make your home movement friendly. Keep frequently used items where you need to reach or bend slightly to get them.

Turn waiting time into movement time. Stretch while watching television. Stand on tiptoe or march in place while brushing your teeth.

Choose the active option. Take stairs when possible. Park a bit further from your destination. Walk to nearby shops.

Modern research confirms what we've learned through experience - regular, moderate activity integrated into daily life can be more beneficial than sporadic intense workouts, especially as we age. It's not about exhausting yourself; it's about staying gently active throughout the day.

We've found that the best movement routine is one that feels natural and enjoyable. For us, it's about finding ways to move that don't feel like exercise at all. Sometimes it's as simple as standing up during phone calls or walking while catching up with friends.

Remember, movement doesn't need to be complicated or strenuous to be effective. The simple act of getting up from your chair multiple times a day, reaching for objects, or walking to the mailbox - these are the movements that keep us independent and mobile well into our nineties.

As we often say, the best exercise program is the one you'll still be doing in your tenth decade. Build movement into your daily routine now, and it will carry you forward for years to come.

The Trap of Doing Too Much

We've seen people injure themselves chasing fitness. They push too hard, too fast, because someone online said sweat equals virtue. It doesn't. The body keeps score — not of your effort, but of your kindness.

Evita: I joined a seniors stretch class once. The instructor shouted, 'Push through the burn!' I quietly ignored her and did what felt right. Later she told me she wished her grandmother could do what I could.

Pain as a Teacher, Not an Enemy

Aging means learning which pain kind of pain warns, and which heals. When our knees ache, they're not scolding us — they're advising moderation. When our backs complain, we check our posture.

We age together, our bodies and us. Partnership, not punishment. Patience above all.

What the Body Remembers

The body keeps score — not just of injury and illness, but of every kindness you've shown it. Treat it gently and it remembers. Neglect it, and it remembers that too.

Our bodies have taught us humility — that we are not invincible; gratitude — that strength is a privilege; and grace — that ageing isn't defeat but a declaration: we've travelled far together.

Every scar, wrinkle, and ache tells a story of endurance and survival. That's what the body remembers most.

Finding Joy in Gentle Physical Activity

The joy of movement doesn't come from pushing limits or breaking records - it comes from finding pleasure in simple, natural activities that keep us strong and independent. Through our nine decades of experience, we've discovered that the most sustainable physical activity is the kind that brings a smile to your face.

Evita: I remember watching Lilian Cox and Doris Hobday demonstrating their chair yoga routines with such delight. As they said, "We enjoy doing chair yoga and showing off. The teachers can't believe how flexible we are for our age." Their playful approach to movement perfectly captures what we've learned - activity should be enjoyable, not punishing.

Lionel: And like Verla and Merla, we've found that creative pursuits naturally incorporate gentle movement. Merla's outdoor painting led her to a profound realization. She started to look at the world a different way, noticing the shapes and colors of rocks and branches on trees. Taking the time to notice things with a wondrous eye will change your life.

We've discovered several key principles for finding joy in gentle activity:

- **Choose activities that feel natural and pleasurable.**

- **Make movement social when possible.**

- **Approach new activities with curiosity.**

- **Find humor and playfulness in motion.**

- **Listen to your body's signals.**

Research supports what we've learned through experience - regular, enjoyable physical activity is linked to increased longevity, particularly when activities are adapted to individual abilities and preferences. The social and emotional elements of shared activity laughter, conversation, shared purpose - are just as important as the physical benefits.

We've found that gentle activities like chair yoga, stretching, gardening, and walking can be sources of both health and happiness when approached with the right mindset. It's not about pushing yourself to exhaustion; it's about finding movements that you look forward to doing each day.

Lionel: I've taken up painting in my later years, and have discovered that it gets me moving in ways I never expected - reaching, bending, walking to find the right view. The movement becomes natural because I'm focused on the joy of creation rather than the exercise itself.

Evita: My contentment comes from gardening and gentle stretching. I don't count repetitions or worry about perfect form. Instead, I focus on how good it feels to reach for a branch or bend to pull out a weed. The movement becomes a celebration of what my body can still do, rather than a reminder of what it can't.

The World Health Organization (WHO) confirms what we've known all along - any activity is better than none, and finding movement you enjoy is key to maintaining it long-term. We've seen countless exercise fads come and go, but the simple pleasure of moving your body never goes out of style.

Remember, gentle physical activity isn't about transformation or performance, it's about maintaining the ability to live independently and finding joy in daily movement. As we often say, the best exercise isn't the one that exhausts you - it's the one that makes you smile while you're doing it.

At ninety-five, we've learned that movement isn't just about exercise - it's about staying engaged with life itself. Through decades of watching fitness trends come and go, we've discovered that the simplest approaches often yield the most lasting results.

Our journey through the decades has taught us that sustainable movement doesn't require expensive equipment or complicated routines. Instead, it's about finding ways to keep the body active that become as natural as breathing. Walking, gardening, household tasks - these aren't just activities, they're investments in longevity.

We've seen how regular, gentle movement sustains not just the body but the spirit. Those who stay mobile into their nineties rarely achieve it through intense workouts or strict regimens. Rather, they maintain their vitality through consistent, mindful movement woven into the fabric of daily life.

Movement as Gratitude

In our youth, exercise was known as chores. We didn't call it fitness — we called it living.

Now, movement feels like thanks.

Each stretch says, Thank you, legs, for still working.

Each deep breath says, Thank you, lungs, for carrying me through.

Movement isn't punishment for eating or a race against time — it's gratitude in motion.

The wisdom we've gained about movement is simple but profound:

- **Move daily, even if just for a few minutes.**

- **Make movement enjoyable rather than punishing.**

- **Listen to your body's natural rhythms.**

- **Choose activities that serve both body and spirit.**

- **Remember that consistency matters more than intensity.**

As we reflect on our journey, we're grateful for every step, every stretch, and every moment of movement that has carried us into our tenth decade. Our bodies may move more slowly now, but they still carry us forward with dignity and grace.

We've learned that the best movement isn't the kind that exhausts you - it's the kind that energizes you to keep going, day after day, year after year. Movement isn't just about adding years to your life; it's about adding life to your years.

So as you close this chapter, remember: Your body is designed for motion. Honor it with regular, gentle movement. Find joy in the simple act of putting one foot in front of the other. Because in the end, it's not about how fast or far you go - it's about keeping going, one step at a time.

Our Rule for Longevity #2:

Move every day - and make it enjoyable enough that you'll want to do it again tomorrow.

CHAPTER 3

Nine Decades of Nourishment

FOOD WISDOM FOR LONGEVITY

Everyone wants to live long, but nobody wants to look like it worked. (Variation of "Every man desires to live long, but no man wishes to be old.")

– Jonathan Swift

The most profound food wisdom we've gathered over ninety years didn't come from diet books or nutrition labels - it came from watching our mother and grandmothers cook with the seasons, family gathered around the table. Food, we learned early on, isn't just about feeding the body; it's about nourishing life itself.

When we were young, 'healthy eating' meant finishing your vegetables before being rewarded with pudding. These days, it seems to require a Master's degree and a laboratory. Everyone's terrified of something - sugar, carbs, dairy, fruit, joy.

We've lived through nine decades of diet trends: grapefruit, cabbage soup, low-fat, low-carb, high-protein, paleo, keto. We've seen them all come and go, often in cycles. Meanwhile we've stayed mostly the same - three light meals a day, plenty of plants, and an open mind toward dessert.

We're not saying that food was always better when we were young. Indeed, there's a far greater selection these days, with wonderful influences from the international community. And we know how to cook food better, not boil the life out of the broccoli or cook the lamb chops until they're charcoal pellets.

Food, to us, has always been about living, not lasting. But we've learned that the two aren't so different. The best way to live long is to eat in a way that sustains not only your body but your spirit.

In this chapter, we'll share our practical wisdom about nourishment - not just what to eat, but how to develop a healthy, sustainable relationship with food that can last a lifetime. We'll explore why simple, whole foods prepared with care have sustained us better than any fad diet or miracle supplement ever could.

We'll discuss how sharing meals builds connections that nourish both body and soul, and why eating should be a pleasure, not a science project. Most importantly, we'll explain why the best diet isn't about restriction - it's about finding joy in food that truly feeds you.

So, pull up a chair to our kitchen table. Let's talk about nine decades of real food wisdom, and how simple nourishment can help you thrive well into your later years.

The Power of Traditional Food Wisdom

Our grandmother used to say that the most powerful medicine often came from the simplest ingredients. She wasn't talking about exotic superfoods or supplements - she meant the nourishing soups, seasonal vegetables, and home-baked breads that sustained our family through good times and lean ones.

When we look back over nine decades of eating, we see that traditional food wisdom wasn't just about what went on the plate - it was about rhythm, ritual, and respect for food itself. Our mother and grandmother knew instinctively what scientists now confirm: that traditional diets based on whole, minimally processed foods are strongly linked to longevity and health.

Core principles that have served us well all our lives:

- **Eat what's in season.** Nature provides what the body needs at the right time - cooling fruits in summer, hearty root vegetables in winter.

- **Waste nothing.** Use everything from the garden. Even vegetable scraps went into the stock pot for soup.

- **Share meals whenever possible.** Food tastes better in company.

- **Cook from scratch.** If you can't pronounce an ingredient, think twice about eating it.

In modern USA, 'cooking from scratch' seems to mean opening a jar of something processed and mixing in a packet of something artificially flavoured, full of sugar, trans-fats and preservatives. No wonder the population is unhealthy, angry and zombie-like. It's running on sugar and chemicals.

These ideas aren't revolutionary - they're time-tested truths that modern science keeps rediscovering. The Mediterranean diet, the Okinawan diet - these aren't trendy eating plans, they're traditional ways of eating that have sustained communities for generations.

We've watched countless food fads come and go, but the basics of good nutrition haven't changed. Fresh vegetables, whole grains, modest portions of meat, fish when you can get it, and treats in moderation - this is the diet that's kept us well into our nineties.

Our friend Margie, who lived to 101, always said her longevity came from eating like her grandmother taught her - simple food, prepared with care, shared with others. She maintained her own vegetable garden well into her nineties, saying the fresh produce and daily tending kept her young. When bending became a strain, she paid a local handyman to have the gardens raised.

We're not against progress or new discoveries about nutrition. But we've noticed that the healthiest elderly people we know aren't following complicated diets or taking handfuls of supplements. They're eating traditional foods, prepared simply, often growing some of their own produce, and most importantly - enjoying their meals without anxiety or guilt.

The wisdom of traditional eating isn't just about nutrition - it's about connection. It's about the ritual of preparing food with care, the pleasure of sharing it with others, and the gratitude for having enough. These aspects of food culture are as important to longevity as any vitamin or mineral.

In our experience, the best diet isn't the most expensive or exotic - it's the one that nourishes both body and soul, the one you can sustain happily for decades. Traditional food wisdom offers exactly that - a way of eating that's both healthy and joyful, tested not in laboratories but in lives well lived.

Mindful Eating and Portion Awareness

Always maintain an interest eating, but don't obsess about it.

When we were young, many of our peers were forced to eat everything on their plates. This was common practise, and part of the "Waste not, want not" mantra. But it also taught many of our generation to overeat. I remember my childhood friend Molly complaining about being forced to eat bread and butter pudding. "We hated it! Stale bread with raisins and a skin of milk on the top. I would be crying and gagging but had to sit at the table until it was finished," she shudders. "Since then, I haven't been able to face bread and butter pudding, even gourmet versions".

Fortunately, our mother did not follow this logic. She simply served smaller portions. She also had a simple way of knowing when to stop eating: she'd put down her fork, smile, and say, "Leave the table wanting just a little more." At the time, we thought she was being overly modest. Years later, we understand the profound wisdom in her gentle approach to portions and mindful eating.

Over nine decades, we've watched portion sizes grow along with waistlines. Restaurant plates have doubled, then tripled. Snack bags that once held a handful now contain enough for a meal. But those who live longest, we've noticed, tend to eat like our grandmother did - slowly, mindfully, and just enough.

The science now confirms what our mother knew intuitively. Studies show that mindful eating - paying attention to our food and eating without distraction - leads to better digestion, improved satisfaction from smaller portions, and ultimately, better health. The Okinawans, famous for their longevity, practice 'hara hachi bu' - eating until they're 80% full, a principle that mirrors our mother's wisdom.

We've maintained simple practices around eating that have served us well:

- **We use smaller plates**, which naturally limit portions.

- **We eat slowly**, using smaller utensils and putting down utensils between bites.

- **We avoid distractions** like television during meals.

- **We avoid sitting idle in front of the television**, keeping our hands busy with crafts and creativity so that our thoughts don't lead to snacking.

- **We stop eating before we feel completely full.**

- **We share meals whenever possible**, which naturally slows down eating.

Our friend Eddie, who lived to 97, always said his secret was "eating like a bird - little bits, often, and never too much at once." He maintained this habit throughout his life, even when others teased him about his modest portions. His vitality into his late nineties suggested he was onto something.

We've found that mindful eating isn't just about how much you eat - it's about how you eat. When you slow down and pay attention, you naturally eat less while enjoying it more. You begin to recognize true hunger from habit, and satisfaction from fullness.

In our youth, post-war rationing taught us to value every morsel. While those were challenging times, they instilled habits of portion awareness that have served us well. We learned to appreciate food rather than simply consume it. Today, we still treat each meal as something special, even if it's just a simple bowl of soup.

The twins Lilian Cox and Doris Hobday exemplified this approach. They enjoyed their favorite foods - even fish and chips - but always in moderation, often sharing a single portion between them. Their philosophy was simple: enjoy what you eat, but never to excess.

We've noticed that those who maintain a healthy weight into their later years aren't usually following strict diets. Instead, they practice what we call 'natural portion control' - eating regular meals, stopping before fullness, and treating food with respect rather than fear or obsession.

Evita: When I finish a meal, I'm thinking about what I'll have for the next one. I plan ahead so I don't reach the "I'm starving" stage and reach for the snacks when I come in from the garden.

Lionel: I also like to think about whether I'm really hungry, or just tired. Is it more food my body wants, or just rest? Sometimes, I'll feel like a snack while watching TV at night. Then I realise, it's not hunger. It's my body reminding me it's time for bed. Sleep is a good distraction from snacking!

Mindful eating also means being present for your meals. We take time to notice the colors, textures, and flavors of our food. We remember to be grateful for each meal, knowing that this appreciation somehow makes even simple food more satisfying.

This approach to eating isn't about restriction - it's about awareness. It's about treating food as nourishment for both body and soul, finding joy in moderation rather than excess. After ninety-five years, we can say with certainty that the pleasure of eating well doesn't come from quantity, but from quality - of the food itself and the attention we give it.

Social Dining and Longevity

The most powerful medicine we've discovered in our ninety-five years isn't found in bottles or supplements - it's found around the dinner table, sharing meals with others. Through nearly a century of living, we've learned that how you eat and who you eat with matters as much as what you eat.

Research now confirms what our grandmothers always knew intuitively - that eating together improves both nutrition and longevity. Studies show that people who share meals regularly tend to eat better, consuming more essential nutrients and making healthier food choices than those who eat alone. But the benefits go far beyond just better nutrition.

Lisa Berkman, Director of the Harvard Center for Population and Development Studies, puts it clearly: "Social isolation carries a risk of mortality that's similar to that of other major risk factors, such as smoking. The stress of isolation can weaken people's immune systems, making them more susceptible to infectious diseases. People with strong social connections tend to have better health behaviors, like eating healthy foods and being physically active."

We see this wisdom reflected in the world's longest-living communities. In Sardinia, Italy, where there's one of the highest concentrations of centenarians globally, daily life revolves around family and community meals. These shared dining experiences aren't just about nutrition - they're about connection, conversation, and community.

Over our decades, we've noticed that those who live longest tend to prioritize social dining. It's not just about the food on the plate - it's about the laughter, stories, and connections shared across the table. When you eat with others, you tend to eat more slowly, digest better, and feel more satisfied with your meal.

Senior nutrition programs have demonstrated this principle clearly. Studies show that older adults who participate in communal dining programs not only eat better but also report greater happiness, reduced loneliness, and enhanced independence. One participant at Wellington Estates captured it perfectly when she said, "It's not just about the food; it's about the laughter and the stories we share. I look forward to every meal."

We've made social dining a priority in our own lives, even as we've grown older. When possible, we share meals with friends or family. When that's not possible, we've found other ways to make meals social - joining community dining programs, organizing small dinner gatherings, or simply sharing tea and a chat with a neighbor.

The health benefits of eating together are remarkable. Research shows that people with strong social connections have a 50% lower risk of premature death compared to those who are isolat.. That's a stronger effect than many medications.

Here are our simple rules for social dining:

- **Make regular meal dates with friends or family.**

- **Join community dining programs when available.**

- **Share recipes and cooking tips with others.**

- **Make mealtimes phone-free zones for better connection.**

- **Don't rush - take time to truly enjoy both the food and the company.**

Even if you live alone, there are ways to make meals more social. Consider joining a lunch club, organizing potluck dinners, or sharing meals with like-minded neighbors. The key is to view dining as an opportunity for connection, not just consumption.

We've found that meals shared with others tend to be more nutritious, more enjoyable, and more memorable than those eaten alone. There's something about breaking bread together that nourishes not just the body, but also the spirit.

In our experience, longevity isn't just about what's on your plate - it's about who's around your table. The simple act of sharing meals creates bonds that strengthen both health and happiness, proving that sometimes the best medicine comes with a side of conversation and companionship. Nine decades into our journey, we've discovered that nourishment isn't just about what's on your plate - it's about how you approach each meal, who you share it with, and the wisdom passed down through generations.

Our mother and grandmothers' simple food principles have proven more valuable than any modern diet trend. Their focus on seasonal eating, minimal waste, shared meals, and cooking from scratch has sustained us well into our nineties. We've watched countless food fads come and go while these timeless truths remain unchanged.

Mindful eating - paying attention to our food and stopping before fullness - has become second nature to us.

Perhaps most importantly, we've discovered that the social aspect of dining has profound effects on both health and happiness. The simple act of sharing meals creates bonds that nourish body and soul alike. Some of our most treasured memories and deepest conversations have happened around the dinner table.

Let's recap the simple lessons we've gathered about nourishment over nine decades:

- **Eat real food**, mostly plants.

- **Cook from scratch** when possible.

- **Share meals** with others.

- **Stop before you're completely full.**

- **Make food a source of joy**, not anxiety.

- **Trust traditional wisdom** over trends.

We've found that the best diet isn't the most complicated or expensive - it's the one that nourishes both body and spirit, the one you can sustain happily for decades. We can say with certainty that good food, eaten mindfully and shared joyfully, is one of life's greatest medicines.

In the end, nourishment isn't about following rules or fads - it's about developing a relationship with food that sustains you for the long haul. It's about finding joy in simple, wholesome meals, sharing them with others, and treating each bite as the gift it truly is.

Our Rule for Longevity #3:

Eat real food. Eat with gratitude. Eat when you're truly hungry and stop before you're full. And never refuse cake on your birthday.

CHAPTER 4

Rhythm and Rest

DAILY HABITS THAT STAND THE TEST OF TIME

The great thing about getting older is that you don't lose all the other ages you've been.

– Madeleine L'Engle

As the evening shadows lengthen across our gardens, Lionel and I have learned to honor the natural signals our bodies send us about rest and renewal. We've discovered that good sleep isn't just about the hours you spend in bed - it's about the rhythm you maintain throughout your entire day. Like an orchestra, every part of life needs its own timing: meals, movement, rest, and activity all playing their parts in harmony.

When people ask us the secret to reaching ninety-five, we often surprise them by talking about sleep and rest. Not supplements or exercise routines, but the gentle power of natural rhythms – the quiet discipline of knowing when to move and when to be still.

Sleep isn't just a pause in living; it's where life renews itself. We've watched countless friends chase longevity through expensive treatments while neglecting this most fundamental medicine of all — proper rest and natural daily rhythms.

This chapter explores how maintaining natural rhythms contributes to longevity more than any modern sleep gadget or supplement. We'll share our practical wisdom about sleep, rest, and the quiet power of routine - lessons learned through nine decades of listening to our bodies' natural signals.

Because in the end, longevity isn't about fighting nature - it's about flowing with it. And that flow begins with understanding the delicate dance between activity and rest, between doing and being.

Let's explore why rest is the most underestimated medicine of all, and how to tune into these natural rhythms that keep us well, starting with the most fundamental rhythm of all - the daily cycle of sleep and wakefulness that has carried us through ninety-five years and counting.

The Power of Consistent Sleep Patterns

The most profound lesson we've learned about sleep isn't from modern science - though that certainly confirms what we've known all along - it's from watching nature's own rhythms. Like the gentle ebb and flow of tides or the predictable cycle of seasons, our bodies crave consistent patterns.

Lionel: I used to pride myself on being able to stay up late, wake early, and power through on minimal rest. Now I know better. The body keeps score, and irregular sleep patterns eventually demand repayment - with interest.

Evita: Our grandmother used to say, "The body repairs itself when you stop meddling with it." She didn't have access to sleep studies or circadian rhythm research, but she understood something fundamental about rest and renewal.

Over nine decades, we've watched countless friends chase expensive sleep solutions - fancy mattresses, sleep tracking devices, elaborate supplements. Meanwhile, we've maintained our health through simple, consistent patterns that align with nature's own rhythm.

Evita: I remember when my friend installed blackout curtains and bought an expensive sleep tracker. She'd wake up anxious about her sleep scores, ironically losing more sleep worrying about sleep. Meanwhile, I was sleeping soundly with my simple routine - a warm drink, a book or audiobook, and the gradual dimming of day into dusk. Sometimes the old ways are the best ways.

Dr. Matthew Walker, a sleep expert we've read about, puts it perfectly: "The shorter your sleep, the shorter your life span." We've seen this play out among our peers. Those who maintained regular sleep patterns generally aged more gracefully than those who treated sleep as an inconvenience.

Another old friend, Lucy, now 92, exemplifies this wisdom. She's maintained the same sleep schedule for decades - in bed by 9:30 PM, up with the sun. "People think I'm rigid," she told us. "But my body thanks me every morning." Her mental clarity and physical vitality speak volumes about the power of consistent rest.

Here's what we've learned about maintaining healthy sleep patterns:

- **Honor your body's natural rhythm.** If you're naturally a morning person, don't fight it. If evening is your time, respect that pattern.

- **Create ritual around rest.** A cup of herbal tea, a few pages of a good book, some gentle stretching - signals that tell your body it's time to wind down.

- **Keep consistent hours, even on weekends.** The body loves predictability.

- **Limit stimulation in the evening hours.** We've noticed that too much excitement - whether from television, conversation, or activity - can disrupt sleep patterns.

The science now confirms what we've learned through experience: regular sleep patterns help regulate everything from metabolism to memory. Dr. Satchin Panda's research shows that maintaining consistent sleep schedules reinforces our circadian rhythms, improving every aspect of health.

But perhaps most importantly, we've learned to respect sleep as medicine, not an inconvenience. When we hear young people boast about getting by on minimal sleep, we think of all the nonagenarians we know. None of them got here by fighting their body's need for rest.

The body whispers before it shouts. Learning to listen to those whispers - the subtle signs of fatigue, the natural ebb of energy as day turns to night - has been one of our most valuable lessons in longevity.

Consistent sleep isn't just about quantity; it's about quality and timing. Like an orchestra, every part of life needs its own rhythm, and sleep is the conductor that keeps everything in harmony.

The Luxury of Sleep

If youth is about chasing mornings, then age is about befriending them. There's a certain grace in slowing down enough to notice the shape of a quiet day. The kettle whistles, the cat yawns, the sunlight lands on the same corner of the table it always has — and suddenly, you realise you're not missing anything by staying still for a while.

Growing old without growing dull isn't about being perpetually busy or relentlessly upbeat. It's about knowing when to move and when to pause, when to seek company and when to savour solitude. Rest, like laughter, has its own intelligence — it keeps the mind supple, the heart steady, and the spirit curious.

Begin Each Day Anew

Evita: Once I leapt out of bed, now I negotiate with it.

When I was in my twenties, mornings were optional. I could tumble out of bed, slap my face with cold water, and be out the door before the kettle had time to sigh.

These days it's more of a negotiation. There's a three-way conversation between my back, my knees, and my sense of humour. One of them always objects.

I've learned not to rush it. The world doesn't collapse if I take an extra five minutes to assemble myself. My younger self would have called it laziness. I call it strategy.

Once negotiations conclude, I put the kettle on, open the curtains, and perform my single most effective act of self-care: I make the bed. It's the day's first victory — proof that I can bring order to at least one corner of the universe.

Lionel: I often have a chuckle about my practical morning ritual, compared with those of wellness influencers versus the nonagenarian's practical version.

I read that some wellness expert starts every day with ice plunges, gratitude journaling, and affirmations. At my age, an ice plunge would qualify as attempted self-harm, and I don't need to write down what I'm grateful for — I remember it every time I open both eyes.

My morning ritual is simpler: sit on the edge of the bed and wait for all my parts to report for duty. The right ankle usually needs coaxing. The shoulders ask for discretion. And my bladder demands priority service.

I don't juice kale; I water the plants and see if I'm still alive. Both are green.

The Late Risers' Club

A friend of ours, Joanie, refuses to get out of bed before ten. She calls it 'slow living.' We call it inertia with branding. She swears the secret to her good skin is horizontal time. We told her our secret is vertical time. We get up, move around, and see what's left of the day to enjoy.

We tease each other mercilessly about our routines. Joanie sends us photos of her breakfast in bed; we send her pictures of the sunrise.

Somewhere between us lies the perfect rhythm of ageing gracefully: not too early, not too late — just on time for your own life.

The Virtue of Sleeping In

Lionel: For decades I used to get up with the birds and I loved it. It always felt like having a head start to the day. I'd feel terribly guilty if I was still in bed at 5am, even in the depths of winter.

When I turned ninety-three, I made a life-altering decision: I disabled my alarm. If the monarch can sleep till nine, so can I. Every morning since, I've woken up whenever my eyelids negotiated peace with the daylight. Some friends still phone before breakfast — old habits die hard — and I let my phone ring. If it's urgent, they'll call back after my dreams are finished.

And why not? There's no medal for beating the sunrise. One of the quiet privileges of ageing is that the clock starts working for you instead of against you. You've earned the right to ignore alarms, roll over, and let the morning light find you when it's ready. The world can wait.

If all this talk of curiosity, novelty and zest feels a bit exhausting, sleep in. Honestly. There's no virtue in bounding out of bed at dawn just to prove you're alive. One of the quiet pleasures of ageing is that the clock starts working for you instead of against you. You've earned the right to ignore alarms, roll over, and let the morning sun filter in at its own pace.

Contrary to the cult of early risers, sleeping in doesn't make you lazy; it makes you rested. Studies show that those who allow themselves flexible sleep — napping when tired, resting when needed — have lower stress hormones like cortisol which interfere with sleep quality and circadian rhythm, especially in older adults. Flexible, restorative sleep patterns improve emotional regulation and resilience. In short, they're less cranky, more content, and far less likely to take on the world's nonsense before coffee.

Sleep isn't a withdrawal from life; it's maintenance for the mind. As we age, we accumulate more memories, worries, and wisdom than our younger selves ever did — all of which need sorting, filing, and pruning while we dream. That's what sleep does best: it resets the emotional circuits, trims the mental clutter, and allows room for the next day's curiosity to bloom.

Besides, lying in bed thinking, remembering, or daydreaming is not wasted time — it's imaginative idling, the kind of mental wandering that sparks creativity and contentment.

Evita: Some mornings, I wake up full of purpose. Other mornings, purpose can wait, and I stay in bed just long enough to think of a reason to get up. It's bliss. I love my bed.

Lionel: Occasionally I'll wake at nine and still feel a bit tired. That's fine. I've waited a long time to have slow, guilt-free mornings. Perhaps that's the real art of longevity: to know that doing less can sometimes mean living more.

Evita: You're not sleeping in, you're marinating.

Mindful Rest and Energy Management

The art of mindful rest isn't about sleeping more - it's about understanding the natural ebb and flow of energy throughout your day. Like the gentle rhythm of ocean tides, our bodies have their own natural cycles of activity and renewal.

Evita: In my younger years, I thought tiredness was a weakness to be conquered. I'd push through fatigue with coffee and willpower, wearing exhaustion like a badge of honor. Now I know better. Rest isn't laziness - it's wisdom.

Lionel: I've learned that energy, like money, needs careful management. Spend it all in the morning, and you'll be bankrupt by noon. The trick is knowing when to invest and when to conserve.

We've watched many friends burn out trying to maintain the same pace they had in their fifties. But longevity isn't about maintaining constant energy - it's about understanding your body's natural rhythms and respecting them.

Our friend Anna exemplifies this perfectly. She used to pride herself on getting by with five hours of sleep, drinking coffee late into the evening and working through the night. Now at 78, she admits that learning to respect her body's natural rhythms was the key to maintaining her vitality. "I stopped fighting my need for rest," she tells us. "And started treating it like the medicine it is."

Here's what we've learned about managing energy wisely:

- **Listen to your body's natural rhythms.** Some hours are for activity, others for rest.

- **Schedule demanding tasks for your peak energy times,** usually morning hours.

- **Take short breaks before you feel exhausted** - prevention is better than recovery.

- **Find restful activities that rejuvenate without depleting** - gentle stretching, reading, or sitting in nature.

The French twins Raymonde and Lucienne, who held the Guinness record for oldest twins, understood this balance well. They maintained their energy through a combination of gentle activities like card games and dancing, interspersed with periods of rest and social enjoyment.

The Rhythm of Rest

Mindful rest isn't just about taking naps (though we're not against those). It's about creating pockets of peace throughout your day. Sometimes it's as simple as sitting quietly for ten minutes, watching the birds in the garden or listening to gentle music.

Evita: I've learned to recognize the early signs of fatigue - when I get twitchy and my mind starts to wander, or small tasks feel over-whelming. That's when I know it's time for what I call my 'restoration breaks.' A cup of tea, a comfortable chair, and permission to simply be still.

Lionel: Learning to listen to your body's whispers of warning - and respond with rest when needed - has been one of my most valuable lessons in longevity.

We've noticed that those who maintain their energy into their nineties aren't the ones who never tire - they're the ones who know how to restore themselves effectively. They understand that rest isn't just the absence of activity - it's an active process of renewal.

This wisdom isn't new - our grandmothers knew it, and their grandmothers too. But in a world increasingly disconnected from natural cycles, one that treats rest as a luxury rather than a necessity, it bears repeating: the body has its own clock, set by sun and seasons, not by schedules and smartphones.

The key is finding your own rhythm - one that honors both your need for activity and your need for renewal. Because in the end, longevity isn't about having boundless energy - it's about having the wisdom to manage the energy you have.

Aligning with Natural Daily Rhythms

The most profound wisdom about daily rhythms comes not from modern science, but from watching nature itself. Like the steady pulse of tides or the predictable arc of seasons, our bodies crave consistent patterns that align with the natural world.

Evita: After ninety-five years, I've learned that fighting these natural rhythms is like swimming upstream - you might manage it for a while, but eventually, the current wins. Our bodies know when to wake, when to rest, when to eat - we just need to start listening again.

Lionel: Modern life often pushes us to ignore these natural signals. We stay up late with artificial light, eat at irregular hours, and push ourselves to be productive when our bodies cry for rest. But longevity isn't about forcing nature - it's about flowing with it.

Through our decades of observation, we've noticed that those who maintain their vitality into their nineties often share one thing in common: they've maintained a natural daily rhythm. They rise and rest with the sun, eat at regular times, and honor their body's need for periodic renewal.

Here's what we've learned about aligning with natural daily rhythms:

- **Wake naturally when possible**, allowing sunlight to signal your body it's time to rise.

- **Eat your main meals at consistent times**, when your digestion is strongest.

- **Honor the natural afternoon lull** instead of fighting it with stimulants.

- **Begin winding down as the sun sets**, allowing your body to prepare for rest.

- **Create quiet evening routines** that ease the transition into sleep.

The body thrives on predictability. When you maintain consistent patterns, everything works better - digestion, sleep, energy, even mood. It's not about rigid schedules; it's about finding your natural rhythm and respecting it.

The most profound lesson about sleep and rhythm isn't just about the hours spent in bed - it's about aligning with nature's own patterns. Like the steady pulse of tides or the predictable arc of seasons, our bodies crave consistent patterns that harmonize with the natural world.

We've watched many friends chase complicated solutions for sleep problems while ignoring the simple power of natural rhythms. Some spent fortunes on sleep gadgets and supplements yet found no peace. Meanwhile, those who maintained consistent patterns - rising with the sun, eating at regular times, honoring the body's need for periodic renewal - often maintained their vitality well into their later years.

The body has its own wisdom - it knows when to be active and when to rest. Our job is simply to listen and align. In doing so, we don't just add years to our life - we add life to our years. Because in the end, longevity isn't about forcing nature - it's about dancing with it, one restful night at a time.

As we close this chapter, remember: Sleep isn't a luxury or an inconvenience - it's the foundation upon which all other aspects of health are built. In our ninety-five years, we've learned that the body repairs itself when you stop meddling with it. Give it the rest it needs, and it will reward you with the energy to truly live.

Our Rule for Longevity #4

This one is simple but profound: Honor your body's natural rhythm. Rest when tired. Sleep as if it's your life's work - because it is.

Remember that fighting these natural patterns is like swimming up-stream - you might manage it for a while, but eventually, the current will win.

Chapter 5

After Retirement and Loss

Keeping a Purpose in Sight

None are so old as those who have outlived enthusiasm.

– Henry David Thoreau

The body needs food and movement, yes, but the spirit needs direction. Without it, the days start to flatten out, and the spark that keeps you alive begins to dim.

We've seen it many times - friends who retired without a plan or interests, convinced they'd earned a life of doing nothing. Within a few years, they were lost, restless, or unwell. It's not that they lacked health - it's that they lacked meaning. The engine was fine, but the driver had lost control of the wheel.

Sadly, many people see their jobs as their identity and are lost without the direction - or perhaps distraction - of a job. Working for decades forces us to manage our precious time for someone else. When left to our own devices we can feel lost or overwhelmed.

Purpose doesn't retire. We may have stopped working decades ago, but we've never stopped working toward something. Purpose doesn't have to be grand. You don't need to save the world; just find something that still feels worth doing. For some, it's a garden. For others, it's family, volunteering, art, or simply showing up for a neighbor.

Evita: After my husband died, I had to find a new reason to get up each day. At first, I didn't have one - grief makes everything grey. Then, little by little, I began tending the citrus trees we'd planted together. I'd prune, water, talk to them. It sounds silly, but it gave me structure. The garden didn't care if I was sad; it just needed me. And in tending to it, I began to tend to myself.

That's the trick with purpose - it often starts small. I love reading and have always been involved in library work. In the back of my mind I have wanted to one day write a book. This is now my purpose.

Lionel: I've always been quite arty and creative, as was our father who enjoyed watercolor painting in his spare time. My first job was in fash-ion, as a window dresser. Eventually I started my own women's wear company which took me all over the world until retirement. As soon as I retired, I started formal art lessons, something I'd always wanted to do yet never been able to make time for. Eventually I built up a little portfolio to exhibit and sell at local galleries. It opened up a whole new world and has given me purpose. I go to bed feeling accomplished and wake up every morning, keen to start a new landscape or embellish an existing one. There are so many things I'd like to paint; I'll need to live for another decade or so!

The Health Benefits Nobody Talks About

Scientists love to measure things - blood pressure, cholesterol, heart rate. But they can't yet measure what purpose does to the human body. We can tell you: it steadies the heart, sharpens the mind, and lifts the immune system. It gives your days contour and your nights peace. It makes you want to eat better, walk farther, and smile more. When you have a reason to live, your body cooperates.

Finding New Purpose After Retirement

People often ask, "But what if I don't know what my purpose is anymore?"

We tell them to start with three small questions:

- **What still brings you joy?** Even a flicker counts.

- **Who still needs you, even in small ways?**

- **What would make tomorrow feel worth getting up for?**

Purpose doesn't always announce itself with trumpets. Sometimes it's as quiet as feeding the cat, writing a letter, or baking scones for the local show. It doesn't need to impress anyone - it just needs to move you forward.

Our friend Jen struggled after retiring from her position as a school administrator. She'd always been known for her organizational skills and leadership, but suddenly those talents seemed to have no outlet. She felt adrift until she started helping at her local community center. "I thought my skills wouldn't be needed anymore," she told us. "But organizing events and mentoring younger volunteers gave me a whole new sense of purpose." Now in her eighties, Jen coordinates multiple community programs and says she's busier - and happier - than ever.

When purpose fades, create it. Write a note, ring a friend you've been thinking about, bake something, read a new book, or plan a walk. Purpose doesn't always find you - sometimes you have to build it with your own two hands. Think of purpose as a muscle. Use it daily, or it fades away. And so do you.

Purpose and gratitude travel together like old friends. Purpose gives direction; gratitude gives light. Together they make each day feel worth living - and that feeling is worth more than any medicine.

Every night, before sleep, name one thing you did that mattered - even if it's tiny. A phone call. A letter. A pot of soup. Then whisper, "That was enough."

And it always is.

The Health Benefits of Meaningful Engagement

The science is clear - having meaningful engagement in life isn't just good for the soul, it's vital medicine for the body and mind. When you have purpose and connection, your whole system responds - heart rate steadies, immune system strengthens, and cognitive function stays sharp well into later years.

We've witnessed this truth firsthand through our friend Raj's remarkable transformation. After retiring from his position as a high school manual arts teacher, his days felt empty and his usual vigor noticeably diminished. He mentioned how much he missed sharing knowledge with young people. "Why does that have to stop?" we asked, suggesting he consider starting an education program at the community centre.

Within months, Raj developed a program teaching both children and seniors about basic manual arts. "I thought retirement meant the end of my purpose," he told us recently. "Instead, it was just the beginning of a new one." Today, at 82, Raj runs three different education programs and mentors other retirees in finding their own post-career purposes.

Research confirms what we've observed - purposeful activity provides profound health benefits. Studies show that regular engagement in mentally challenging activities improves cognitive function and may delay age-related decline. Even gentle physical movement incorporated into meaningful activities contributes to flexibility and mobility. Perhaps most importantly, maintaining close relationships and active participation in family or community life strongly correlates with both longevity and psychological wellbeing.

The emotional benefits are equally powerful. Pursuing hobbies, crafts, or learning new skills fosters pride and satisfaction that directly boost mood and resilience. Sharing laughter, stories, and enjoyment with others has been consistently linked to lower rates of depression and anxiety among older adults. Having someone to talk to daily and maintaining close ties helps mitigate the negative effects of isolation or loss.

The key is finding engagement that combines social connection with a sense of contribution.

This could mean:

- **Taking classes or learning new skills.**

- **Volunteering at community organizations.**

- **Pursuing creative activities like art or music.**

- **Mentoring others and sharing your wisdom.**

- **Participating in social/faith groups or civic organizations.**

The form your engagement takes matters less than ensuring it gives you purpose and connection. Start small, stay consistent, and notice how your body and spirit respond to having meaningful ways to contribute and connect. Because when you have something that matters to wake up for each day, your whole system aligns to support that purpose.

As we often say - it's not about doing everything, it's about doing something that matters to you. The world still needs what only you can give. And your body needs the vitality that comes from staying meaningfully engaged in life.

Creating Legacy Through Daily Actions

Legacy isn't something you leave behind - it's something you build every day through small, consistent actions that ripple outward to touch others' lives. After nine decades of watching how influence spreads, we've learned that the most powerful legacies often grow from the quietest seeds.

Evita: I used to think legacy meant grand gestures or achievements - writing a book, building a business, leaving wealth for the next generation. But watching our late sister Laura face devastating loss in her eighties taught me otherwise. After losing both her partner and retirement savings, she had to downsize from her beloved home of fifty years to a small apartment. Instead of being broken by these circumstances, she transformed her new space into a cozy haven filled with her most cherished possessions and memories. "You know," she told me, "I've discovered that happiness isn't about having everything - it's about appreciating what remains." Her ability to find purpose and joy amid loss became her true legacy, teaching all who knew her about resilience and grace.

The daily practice of legacy building is made through simple, consistent actions:

- **Embracing humor and positivity,** even in difficult times.

- **Nurturing genuine connections** with others.

- **Staying adaptable** and open to learning new things.

- **Finding joy in life's simple pleasures** and sharing that joy with others.

These aren't grand gestures, but they create ripples that touch countless lives. When we demonstrate resilience, gratitude, or kindness in our daily interactions, we show others what's possible at any age.

Lionel: I never expected that starting art lessons in my retirement would inspire others. But watching younger retirees take up painting after seeing my small gallery shows taught me that every action, no matter how personal, can light the way for someone else.

Authenticity has become our most powerful legacy. By living genuinely and openly sharing our vulnerabilities, adapting to changes, and finding joy in simple pleasures, we give others permission to do the same. Legacy isn't about being perfect - it's about being real.

We've learned that legacy building happens in small moments:

- **Taking time to truly listen** to someone who needs to talk.

- **Sharing wisdom when asked,** but also admitting when we don't know.

- **Showing up consistently** for the people and causes we care about.

- **Demonstrating that it's never too late** to learn, grow, or begin again.

Every day offers new opportunities to contribute to the world in meaningful ways. Whether through mentoring others, sharing stories, or simply modeling resilience and joy, we're constantly weaving our legacy through our daily choices and actions.

The beauty of this approach is that it takes the pressure off creating some grand legacy and instead focuses on living each day with intention and authenticity. Because in the end, the most powerful legacy isn't what we leave behind - it's how we inspire others to live while we're here.

Making Purpose a Priority

Looking back over this chapter, we see how purpose threads through every moment of a long and well-lived life. It's not just about having something to do - it's about having something that matters, something that makes each day worth greeting.

Through stories like Raj finding renewed meaning in teaching manual arts after retirement, and our own journeys of discovering new passions, we've witnessed how purpose doesn't retire - it simply evolves. Whether it's tending a garden through grief, taking up painting in our later years, or writing to share our experiences, having direction and meaning contributes profoundly to both physical and mental wellbeing.

While science may not be able to measure purpose in blood tests or brain scans, its effects are undeniable. We've watched it steady hearts, sharpen minds, and lift spirits time and time again. When you have something meaningful to wake up for, your whole body responds - you eat better, move more, sleep deeper.

Perhaps most importantly, we've learned that purpose doesn't have to be world-changing or recognised. It can be as simple as caring for a garden, teaching a skill, or being there for someone who needs you. The key is finding something that combines meaning with contribution, something that makes tomorrow worth greeting.

For those still searching for their post-retirement purpose, remember our three guiding questions: What still brings you joy? Who still needs you, even in small ways? What would make tomorrow feel worth getting up for?

Purpose, like a river, finds new channels as life changes. Sometimes it flows strong and clear; other times it needs to carve new paths. But as long as it keeps moving, keeps seeking, keeps finding its way forward, it continues to nourish and sustain.

As we close this chapter, remember that having purpose isn't just about living longer - it's about living better, right up to the very end. When we have something meaningful to wake up for, someone to care for, and something to look forward to, each day becomes a gift rather than a burden.

Our Rule for Longevity #5:

Have something to wake up for, someone to care for, and something to look forward to - even if it's just tomorrow's stunning sunrise and birdsong.

Chapter 6

The Company You Keep

Connections That Count

I will never be an old man. To me, old age is always fifteen years older than I am.

– Francis Bacon

The adage, 'you are the company you keep', has proven itself true throughout our long lives, not just in terms of character but in its profound impact on health and longevity. Like the intertwining branches of the old crepe myrtle in the garden, supporting each other through storms, our social connections form a living network that sustains us through life's challenges.

We've come to believe that people don't die of old age so much as they die of isolation. The body can survive a great many things, but the soul cannot thrive in loneliness.

The research is clear - social connections play a crucial role in both emotional health and longevity. Strong social bonds have been shown to reduce the risk of premature death and protect against various age-related diseases. We've seen this truth played out countless times in our own lives and those of our peers.

Evita: I've always loved my own company whereas Lionel has always been more social. I love pottering around, lost in my thoughts. Socialising can sometimes feel overwhelming to me. I rarely feel lonely when I'm alone, but even the most introverted or reclusive person needs a human connection occasionally.

In my ninety-five years, I've watched strong, healthy people fade once they became disconnected — and frail ones blossom again once someone made them feel seen. Companionship is a medicine that doesn't come in bottles. And I don't mean another partner, my husband was irreplaceable. Just the occasional chat, laugh or company. Connection.

You can't buy friendship, and you can't fake belonging. That's why no longevity 'expert' talks about it much — there's no product to sell. But if you look at the world's longest-living communities, they all share one thing: connection.

People eat together, work together, care for one another. They celebrate, mourn, and grow old side by side. They have names for one another, histories, and small rituals that mean they matter.

That's what keeps the spirit alive — knowing you're woven into a web that would miss you if you weren't there.

In this chapter, we'll explore how these vital connections - from deep friendships to casual conversations - contribute not just to longevity, but to the quality of those extra years. We'll share our experiences of maintaining relationships through life's changes, and practical wisdom for staying meaningfully connected as the world around us transforms.

Because at ninety-five, we've learned that the warmth of human connection does more than comfort - it sustains, it heals, and it gives each day its meaning. Let's discover how to nurture these life-giving bonds, one conversation at a time.

Maintaining Social Connections in Later Years

The art of maintaining social connections in our later years requires both intention and adaptability. As we age, our social circles naturally shift - some friends move away, others pass on, and family dynamics evolve. Yet the need for meaningful connection remains as vital as ever.

Lionel: I've learned that social connections are like a garden - they need effort and regular tending. You can't just plant once and expect things to flourish. You must water, prune, and sometimes replant entirely.

Evita: I've discovered that maintaining connections doesn't always mean grand gestures or elaborate plans. Sometimes it's as simple as a regular phone call, a weekly coffee date, or joining a local community group. The key is consistency and genuine interest in others.

Here are the practices we've found most helpful in nurturing social connections:

- **Make the first move.** Don't wait for invitations - extend them. Even if you're not feeling particularly social, reach out. The effort itself often lifts your spirits.

- **Embrace technology selectively.** While we don't need every new gadget, learning to use video calls and simple messaging can help bridge physical distances, especially with family.

- **Create regular rituals.** Whether it's a weekly card game, a morning walking group, or monthly community meetings, having scheduled social activities provides structure and anticipation.

- **Stay curious about others.** Ask questions, remember details about people's lives, and follow up on their stories. Genuine interest in others keeps relationships fresh and meaningful.

- **Accept help gracefully.** Sometimes maintaining connections means allowing others to assist you - it gives them purpose and strengthens bonds.

One of the most valuable lessons we've learned about social connection came from observing our friend Fran. Not only did she regain purpose, but she was also able to combat her loneliness following the loss of her husband.

Grieving, Fran had withdrawn from social activities. Her health began to decline rapidly - not just from grief, but from isolation. After stepping out of her comfort zone and taking the brave step of starting her social group, Fran's blood pressure improved, her mobility increased, and her spirit lifted. The medical research explains why - social connection triggers the release of hormones that reduce stress and promote healing.

The science supports what we've learned through experience - strong social connections contribute significantly to longevity and well-being in later years. Studies consistently show that socially engaged older adults demonstrate better cognitive function, stronger immune systems, and greater emotional resilience.

But perhaps most importantly, social connections give our days texture and meaning. They provide reasons to get dressed, to laugh, to share stories, and to feel part of something larger than ourselves.

Evita: I've noticed that the quality of connections matters more than quantity. It's better to have a few meaningful relationships than many superficial ones. I maintain close friendships with people of various ages - each bringing different perspectives and energy to my life.

Lionel: And remember, connection isn't just about conversation. Sometimes it's about shared silence, a game of cards, or simply being in the same room while reading different books. The presence of others can be as comforting as their words.

We've found that maintaining social connections requires both flexibility and persistence. As mobility changes, we may need to adapt how we socialize. Perhaps the weekly walk becomes a seated chat, or the dinner party becomes an afternoon tea. The key is to focus on what's still possible rather than what's been lost.

Most importantly, never underestimate the power of simple human contact. A smile exchanged with a neighbor, a brief chat with the postal carrier, or a phone call to an old friend - these small moments of connection weave together to create a tapestry of belonging that sustains us through our later years.

The Health Benefits of Meaningful Relationships

Research has consistently shown what we've known intuitively all along - meaningful relationships are as vital to our health as any medicine or exercise routine. We've watched countless studies confirm what our own nine decades of experience have taught us: people with strong social ties tend to live longer, healthier lives.

Evita: The evidence is written in the faces of those who've lived longest - they're rarely the isolated ones. They're the ones who maintain connections, who laugh often, who have someone to share their stories with. I've seen it in our retirement community - those who stay connected, even if just through regular chats with a trusted neighbor or weekly calls with family, tend to thrive.

Lionel: It's fascinating how science now confirms what our mother always knew. She used to say, "A shared cup of tea is better medicine than any tonic." Modern research shows she was right - strong social ties can reduce the risk of everything from heart disease to cognitive decline.

The health benefits of meaningful relationships are remarkable:

- **Reduced risk of depression and anxiety.**

- **Better cognitive function and slower mental decline.**

- **Increased likelihood of engaging in healthy behaviors.**

- **Greater resilience when facing health challenges.**

- **Lower blood pressure and stronger immune systems.**

The Harvard Study of Adult Development, which has tracked people for over 75 years, confirms what we've observed: good relationships keep us happier and healthier. As Dr. Robert Waldinger, the study's director, noted, "Good relationships are better predictors of long and happy lives than social class, IQ, or even genes."

But it's not just about having people around - it's about the quality of those connections. We've noticed that meaningful relationships, where you can be yourself and feel truly heard, provide the greatest benefits. A few close friends who really know you are worth more than a hundred casual acquaintances.

Lionel: I remember when our friend Eddie, who prided himself on being a loner, had a health scare at 85. His recovery was notably faster once he allowed his neighbors to help with meals and companionship. The simple act of having someone to talk to each day seemed to accelerate his healing.

Evita: And it's not just about receiving support - giving it matters too. When I volunteer at the local library's reading program, I come home feeling energized. Science explains this as well - helping others triggers positive physiological changes in our bodies.

The research is clear - lacking social connection can be as damaging to health as smoking 15 cigarettes a day. It's not just about loneliness - it's about the fundamental human need for connection and its profound impact on our physical well-being.

So, our advice? Don't treat relationships as a luxury - they're a necessity. Make time for them. Nurture them. Your health depends on it as much as any vitamin or exercise routine. Because at our age, we can tell you -

the warmth of human connection is one of the most powerful medicines we have.

Creating and Nurturing Supportive Communities

The art of building supportive communities isn't just about having people around - it's about creating meaningful connections that sustain us through life's challenges. We've learned this truth through nine decades of watching communities form, evolve, and strengthen.

Evita: When I think about the communities that have sustained me, I'm reminded of the Tipton Twins who lived next door to each other well into their nineties. Like them, Lionel and I have found that physical proximity enables those spontaneous moments of connection that weave the fabric of community.

Lionel: Yes, and like those twins, we've discovered that community isn't just about family - it's about creating a network of mutual support that extends beyond blood ties. It's about having people who notice when you haven't been seen for a day, who share their garden's bounty, or who simply stop for a chat.

Here are the essential elements we've found for creating and nurturing supportive communities:

- **Start where you are.** Join local groups, attend community events, or simply be present in shared spaces.

- **Make regular connections.** Whether it's a weekly coffee group or daily walks with a good friend.

- **Share skills and knowledge.** Teach what you know, learn from others.

- **Embrace technology thoughtfully.** Use it to maintain connections, not replace them.

- **Create rituals of togetherness.** Regular shared meals, hobby groups, or simple check-ins.

We've observed that the strongest communities often grow from simple, consistent interactions. Take our friend Shirl, another nonagenarian twin who shared with us how living and laughing together with her sister has sustained them both: "We talk and laugh and share stories. We laugh. All that helps."

The science confirms what we've learned through experience - strong community ties contribute significantly to longevity. Research shows that people with robust social networks tend to live longer, healthier lives. But it's not just about having people around - it's about the quality of those connections.

Lionel: I've noticed that the most resilient communities are those that embrace both giving and receiving. When I was recovering from hip surgery, my neighbors organized a meal roster. Later, I taught several of them how to propagate plants from cuttings. This reciprocity strengthens the bonds between us.

Evita: And during times of crisis, like the recent pandemic, we saw how vital these community connections become. We've seen how flexible, adaptable communities can provide crucial support when needed most.

The key to building lasting community ties is authenticity. Share your real self - your joys, your concerns, your humor. We've found that genuine connections, even if fewer in number, serve us better than many superficial ones.

Here's what we've learned about maintaining community bonds:

- **Stay curious** about others' lives (there's a difference between interest and nosiness).

- **Celebrate shared victories,** no matter how small.

- **Show up consistently** for others.

- **Accept help gracefully** when offered.

- **Keep humor** and lightness in your interactions.

Remember, building community isn't about grand gestures - it's about small, consistent actions that create lasting connections. Whether it's sharing a cup of tea, exchanging garden produce, or simply stopping for a chat, these everyday moments build the foundation of lasting support networks.

Our communities may change shape as we age, but their importance never diminishes. In fact, as we get older, these connections become even more vital to our well-being and happiness. They provide not just practical support, but the emotional sustenance that makes each day worth living.

The Power of Real Connection

As we conclude this chapter on the vital importance of social connections, we're reminded of a truth that nine decades of living has confirmed: relationships and community aren't just nice to have - they're essential to both longevity and life quality.

Through our personal experiences, scientific understanding, and observations of countless lives, we've seen how meaningful connections act as both anchor and sail - keeping us grounded while helping us move forward through life's changes.

The evidence is clear - both in research and in the faces of those who've lived longest. Those who maintain strong social bonds, who laugh often, who have someone to share their stories with - these are the ones who tend to thrive into their later years. No supplement or exercise routine can replace the healing power of human connection.

We've learned that creating and maintaining these vital connections requires intention but not complexity. Simple actions - a regular phone call, a weekly coffee date, a shared hobby - can weave a strong social fabric that supports us through our later years.

Remember:

- **Quality matters more than quantity in relationships.**

- **Consistency in connection matters more than grand gestures.**

- **Both giving and receiving support strengthens social**

bonds.

- **Technology can bridge physical distances when used thoughtfully.**

- **It's never too late to build new connections.**

Evita: Looking back over ninety-five years, I can say with certainty that the warmth of human connection has been as vital to my longevity as any health practice. The laughter shared with friends, the quiet companionship of family, even brief exchanges with the next-door neighbor - these moments have given texture and meaning to my days.

Lionel: And I've noticed how those who maintain strong social connections seem to weather life's challenges better. They recover more quickly from illness, adapt more easily to change, and find more joy in daily life.

As you move forward, remember that nurturing relationships isn't just about adding years to your life - it's about adding life to your years. Make time for connection. Reach out first. Accept invitations. Share your stories. Because at ninety-five, we can tell you with certainty - the company you keep shapes not just your character, but your very chances of a long and fulfilling life.

In the next chapter, we'll explore another vital aspect of longevity - keeping your mind sharp through the years. But for now, consider this: Who will you reach out to today? What connection will you nurture? Your health - and your happiness - may depend on it.

Our Rule for Longevity #6:

Keep good company - it will lengthen your life and sweeten your day.

Chapter 7

The Nonagenarian Mind

Staying Sharp Through the Years

I'm not old; I'm chronologically gifted.

– Unknown

People often say the mind is like a muscle, but after ninety-five years, we've learned it's more like a garden – it needs constant tending, to stay vibrant and productive, not just occasional bursts of attention.

After decades of cultivating our mental landscapes, we've learned that curiosity isn't just a trait; it's a practice that keeps the mind fertile and growing.

The greatest threat to mental vitality isn't age itself, but rather the assumption that aging means inevitable decline.

Lifelong Learning and Curiosity

Evita: I still ask questions. Sometimes they're silly, sometimes profound. "Why do birds never seem tired?" "How does Wi-Fi travel through walls?"

Curiosity gives you a reason to pay attention. When you stop wondering, you start withdrawing.

That's why I read, listen to podcasts, watch documentaries, and ask my grandchildren to explain the world to me. They've helped me set up and maintain an active online presence and learn new platforms. They light up when they teach me something new, and I light up from learning it. My daily engagement with social media and technology keeps my mind sharp and keeps me connected with younger generations. It's proof that age is no barrier to learning new skill if you're open to learning them.

The day I stop learning, I'll start shrinking - and I have no interest in becoming smaller.

Lionel: You have to keep learning. Every decade or so, I've made a rule to learn something that challenges me. At seventy, it was croquet. At eighty, it was online banking and Google. At ninety, I started exploring Artificial Intelligence. I may never fully understand it, but how I enjoy trying. It's like cracking a code. I hope I'm still around for the next big thing!

Daily engagement with social media and technology keeps the mind sharp. The sharpest nonagenarians maintain active online presences, learn new platforms, and connect with younger generations - proving that age is no barrier to keeping the mind open, and to learning new skills.

Blythe, a bridge partner of thirty years, had always prided herself on her sharp memory and quick wit. When she turned eighty-five, she began noticing small changes in her recall and became increasingly anxious about cognitive decline. During one of our weekly games, we shared our own experience with maintaining mental agility through continuous learning. Six months later, Blythe was teaching other seniors how to use social media to connect with their grandchildren.

Think Stimulation, Not Mastery

The trick isn't mastery; it's stimulation. When your brain works to understand something new, it's literally building fresh connections. Neuroscientists call it 'plasticity.' We call it keeping the lights on upstairs.

So, whatever your age - learn something new. Take up an instrument. Study a language. Write a poem. Challenge your brain and keep pushing those boundaries a little every day. Your mind will thank you with continued vitality and engagement.

The best brain workout we know is conversation. Real conversation, not small talk. Debating, storytelling, remembering together - all of it wakes the mind. A chat with a sharp friend keeps you sharper too. Listening is exercise; so is laughter.

We've found that learning alongside others multiplies the benefits. Whether it's a book club, a painting class, or simply discussing current events, shared learning strengthens both mind and social bonds. These connections provide emotional support, which research shows is essential for mental well-being.

Remember, curiosity isn't about having all the answers. It's about staying interested in the questions. That's what keeps the mind young - not the knowing, but the wondering.

Mental Exercise Through Daily Challenges

Every morning, we challenge our minds with small but meaningful tasks - not because we're trying to become geniuses, but because we've learned that daily mental exercise is as vital as physical movement for longevity. Like tending a garden, the mind needs regular care, not just occasional bursts of attention.

Lionel: I've made it a habit to tackle the daily crossword, not because I always finish it, but because the process of trying keeps my mind nimble. Sometimes I'll deliberately take a different route to the shops or try to recall the names of everyone I met at yesterday's bridge club. These aren't grand challenges, but they're consistent ones.

Evita: My approach involves mixing routine with novelty. I do familiar tasks in new ways - like brushing my teeth with my non-dominant hand or calculating the grocery bill in my head before reaching the checkout. Small changes that keep the mind alert.

We've found that the best mental exercises are those embedded in daily life:

- **Learning one new fact each morning** from Google, the newspaper or a podcast.

- **Memorizing a short poem or quote each week.**

- **Playing strategic games** like chess or bridge with friends.

- **Teaching others something we know well,** which requires organizing our thoughts clearly.

- **Engaging in conversations that challenge** our perspectives.

Perhaps most importantly, we've learned to approach these challenges with playfulness rather than pressure. It's not about scoring points or proving anything - it's about keeping the mind flexible and engaged.

We've seen too many peers give up on mental challenges because they fear making mistakes. But that's exactly backward - it's the willingness to be wrong, to learn, to try again that keeps the mind young.

The science supports what we've learned through experience - that cognitive reserve, built through daily mental challenges, helps protect against age-related decline. It's like building a savings account for your mind - every small deposit of mental activity adds up over time.

We particularly enjoy activities that combine social interaction with mental stimulation. Our weekly bridge club isn't just about the card game - it's about strategy, memory, and lively conversation. These social-cognitive activities create multiple benefits: they exercise the mind while maintaining vital social connections.

Remember, the goal isn't to become a genius at ninety-five. It's to keep the mind flexible, curious, and engaged. Like physical exercise, mental challenges should leave you energized, not exhausted. Start small, stay consistent, and most importantly, make it enjoyable enough that you'll want to continue.

As we often say: The mind doesn't wear out from use - it wears out from lack of use. So, give it something interesting to think about every single day.

Cognitive Resilience Through Social Engagement

The most powerful tool for maintaining cognitive vitality isn't found in brain training apps or expensive supplements - it's found in the company we keep and the connections we nurture. Through nine decades of living, we've witnessed how social engagement acts as both shield and stimulant for the mind.

Evita: When people ask how we've kept our minds sharp into our nineties, they often expect to hear about crossword puzzles or memory games. But we also tell them about our little technological feats, and the young neighbors who keep us updated on popular culture. These connections challenge our thinking, spark our curiosity, and give us reasons to stay engaged with the world.

Lionel: I've noticed that the sharpest nonagenarians I know aren't necessarily the ones doing the most brain exercises - they're the ones who maintain rich social lives. They're involved in their communities, have regular conversations with people of different ages, and stay connected to what's happening in the world.

We've seen this truth reflected in the lives of other long-lived twins, like Lilian Cox and Doris Hobday, who remained mentally vibrant into their mid-90s through active social engagement. They even embraced social media in their nineties, connecting with younger generations and sharing their experiences online. Their story shows how new forms of social connection can keep the mind adaptable and engaged at any age.

The science supports what we've observed - regular social interaction doesn't just make life more enjoyable, it helps build cognitive resilience. Like a mental gymnasium, every conversation exercises different parts of the brain - memory, language, emotional regulation, and executive function.

Here's what we've learned about building cognitive resilience through social connection:

- **Maintain diverse social circles** that include people of different ages.

- **Engage in activities** that combine social interaction with mental challenge, like card games or book clubs.

- **Share stories and memories** - it exercises recall while strengthening bonds.

- **Stay current with technology** that helps you connect with family and friends.

- **Embrace opportunities to learn from others**, especially younger generations.

During the COVID-19 lockdown, we witnessed how vital social connections are for mental resilience. Those who maintained regular contact with others, even virtually, seemed to fare better cognitively than those who became isolated.

Evita: I remember how the twins Lilian and Doris described their lockdown experience as a '5-star hotel' atmosphere because they had each other and family support. It showed us how protective social bonds can be during challenging times.

Staying Open to Connection

We've learned that cognitive resilience isn't just about preserving what we have - it's about growing through our connections with others. Every new conversation, shared laugh, or fresh perspective helps keep our minds flexible and engaged.

The beauty of social engagement is that it's available to everyone, regardless of education or resources. A friendly chat with a neighbor, a phone call with family, or joining a community group - these simple interactions build cognitive strength as surely as any formal brain training program.

So, while crossword puzzles have their place, we believe the best exercise for the aging mind is the warmth of human connection. It's not just about staying sharp - it's about staying connected to the flow of life itself. As we reflect on the wisdom gathered from nine and a half decades of keeping our minds sharp and engaged, we're reminded that mental vitality isn't about following complicated regimens or expensive programs - it's about maintaining curiosity, connection, and continual growth.

The greatest lesson we've learned about cognitive health is that the mind thrives not on perfection, but on persistence. And most importantly, it needs engagement with life itself.

Through our journey, we've discovered that mental vitality comes from:

- **Staying curious about the world around us.**

- **Engaging in regular social interaction.**

- **Embracing new learning opportunities.**

- **Maintaining a sense of purpose.**

- **Finding joy in daily challenges**

Remember that keeping your mind sharp isn't about competing with others or even with your younger self. It's about staying engaged, interested, and open to new experiences. Whether it's learning a new language, mastering technology, or simply having meaningful conversations, every mental challenge helps build cognitive resilience.

Perhaps most importantly, we've learned that mental vitality isn't separate from emotional and physical health - they're all interconnected. A walk with a friend exercises both body and mind. A good laugh strengthens both heart and brain. A new challenge builds both confidence and cognitive reserve.

As we close this chapter, we invite you to embrace mental exercise not as a duty, but as an adventure. Your mind is not a machine to be maintained, but a garden to be cultivated - with patience, curiosity, and joy.

Our Rule for Longevity #7:

Feed your curiosity daily, stretch your mind often, and never stop being interested in the world - it will stay interested in you.

CHAPTER 8

Growing Old

WITHOUT GROWING DULL

In youth we learn; in age we understand.

– Marie von Ebner-Eschenbach

As we age, there's a sneaky danger that creeps up—not arthritis or forgetfulness, but something far more socially perilous: becoming a bore.

It often happens without malice or awareness. We start telling stories not because anyone asked, but because the silence feels too long or the memory feels too good to keep to ourselves. Before we know it, we've launched into a detailed account of "how things used to be," complete with side plots about petrol prices in 1973. The trouble isn't that our stories aren't worth telling—they are—but that we sometimes forget to notice whether anyone's still listening.

Let's face it—older people can be dreadful bores. We've all met the kind: the uncle who corners you at a barbecue and tells the same war story for the twentieth time, or the neighbor who recounts her gallbladder surgery in forensic detail.

Age does not automatically make one interesting. It can, if we're not careful, make us tedious. The more we live, the more material we have—but that doesn't mean that everyone wants to hear it.

A lifetime of memories can easily turn into a monologue if we forget to notice when the listener's eyes glaze over.

Staying Interested and Interesting

This tendency to drone on often comes from a good place. We want to share what we've learned, to connect, to feel that our lives meant something.

There's comfort – at least for the teller - in the familiar rhythms of a well-worn story. It reassures us that we've been through things, survived them, and come out wiser.

But be mindful of causing discomfort to your listeners, who are probably trying to back away slowly.

There's a fine line between sharing wisdom and performing a one-person nostalgia show. If we don't stay curious about others, our stories stop being bridges and start being walls.

Evita: A gentle reminder to stay rooted in the now. Don't live in the past; visit it occasionally, but keep your bags packed for the present.

The real trick to growing old without growing dull is knowing when to stop talking—and start asking questions.

Conversation should be a dance, not a lecture. Yet too many older people treat it like a history lesson, complete with dates, names, and unnecessary footnotes.

It's not that our memories are unworthy; it's that the delivery often lacks awareness. The best stories—at any age—have freshness, humour, and humility. They're told with an eye for what will resonate now, not what mattered decades ago. If your audience is smiling politely while checking their phone, or showing signs of a panic attack, it's time to trim the anecdote or let it rest in peace.

The good news is that self-awareness is the cure for conversational dullness. A lively old age isn't about keeping quiet; it's about keeping relevant. Tell stories by all means—but choose them the way you'd choose wine: selectively, thoughtfully, and suited to the occasion.

Ask yourself, "Does this add something to the moment?" If not, it's better saved for a journal than a dinner table. Because nothing makes you seem younger and more vibrant than genuine curiosity about others and a sense of timing about yourself.

In the end, nobody minds hearing your stories—if you tell them well, briefly, and with a twinkle in your eye. And preferably only once. What people mind is being trapped in a conversational time capsule. So edit your anecdotes, update your references, and leave a little mystery. After all, the most interesting older people aren't the ones who've seen the most—they're the ones who still see you.

Stay fresh and keep moving forward. Stay interesting and interested with just the right amount of reverence. Be the person who asks good questions, not the one who answers unasked ones. Keep your mind on wander, not repeat.

The secret to staying young is curiosity, not chronology. Focus on the mindset that keeps one youthful regardless of age.

Lionel: Stories age well only when their tellers don't. Stay curious, not curmudgeonly.

Evita: If your story takes longer than drinking a cup of tea, save it for your memoirs.

The stories we've gathered over a lifetime are treasures, but even treasures can gather dust if we don't keep them moving. Share them, yes—but also make room for new ones.

The world keeps changing, and so can we. Ask the young what they're reading, try to understand a meme even if it makes no sense, and let yourself be surprised by the small things—a new café, a strange gadget, a neighbour's grandchild with blue hair and bold opinions. Staying lively isn't about pretending to be young; it's about refusing to close the door on wonder.

The Myth of the Dull Old Person

Ageing, for all its surprises, needn't be an exercise in dullness. Yet somewhere along the way, we confused getting older with getting beige — sensible shoes, muted tones, quiet opinions. We've been told to "act our age" so often that many people take it as an instruction to dim the lights of their personality. But the truth is, curiosity, mischief and wit don't expire; they just need a little oxygen.

Let's get this straight: dullness isn't a function of age; it's a function of disengagement. You can meet an 85-year-old who's crackling with ideas and a 35-year-old who's already coasting in neutral.

What makes us interesting is interest itself — in people, ideas, music, politics, weather, gossip, gardens, grandkids, or galaxies.

Neuroscience backs this up. The brain's dopamine pathways — responsible for motivation and reward — respond not only to novelty but also to anticipation. The mere thought of learning or doing something new releases a tiny hit of pleasure chemistry. That's why trying a new recipe or planning a trip gives you a lift. And the older we get, the more our brains rely on these small sparks to keep the circuitry humming.

The Spark of Curiosity

Lionel: The day I stop being curious, check for a pulse.

Our friend June, 91, decided during lockdown to learn Italian on her iPad. "I can't remember all the verbs," she admits, "but I do remember feeling alive again." She doesn't plan to visit Rome; she just enjoys the stretch. Curiosity, for her, isn't about mastery — it's about movement.

Another friend, Bernie, 87, began painting at 80 after his wife's passing. "I'd never held a brush," he said, "but grief needed colour." He now sells small watercolours at the local market and has become, to his astonishment, 'the artsy one' of his family.

These are not people escaping age — they're inhabiting it fully. They understand that dullness is the real danger, not decline.

The Psychology of Freshness

Psychologists have found that older adults who regularly try new things — no matter how small — show improved mood, memory, and emotional resilience. It's called the novelty effect, and it works whether you're learning a dance step, joining a reading group, or switching to oat milk just to see what the fuss is about.

The key is movement of the mind. We stagnate not when our knees creak, but when our curiosity does. The world remains interesting as long as we do.

Hugh's Second Act

When Hugh retired from teaching physics, he stopped shaving for six months and stopped smiling for two years. His daughter finally dragged him to a community theatre audition — a small part, no lines. He protested, then went along, "just to watch."

Two months later, he was cast as a grumpy postmaster in a local comedy. "I didn't have to act much," he joked. But something changed. He started laughing again. He had new friends, new lines to learn, new cues to miss.

Now 89, Hugh has appeared in seven productions. "I thought I was done," he says. "Turns out, I was just between acts."

How Not to Grow Dull

- **Stay curious.** Ask questions. The world is an endless unfolding — not a finished story.

- **Be a beginner.** Try things you're not good at. Humility keeps you interesting.

- **Keep your opinions flexible.** Stiff thinking ages faster than stiff joints.

- **Mix with all ages.** The young lend energy, and you lend perspective.

- **Laugh at the absurdity of it all.** Nothing rejuvenates like the ability to find life funny — especially your own life.

The Science of Zest

The psychologist Paul Baltes, who studied successful ageing, found that openness to experience — a willingness to engage with new people, ideas and emotions — predicts not just happiness, but cognitive vitality. In other words, the more open you are, the more alive your brain stays.

This openness doesn't mean forced optimism or pretending everything is wonderful. It means keeping your windows unlatched — letting in air, light, surprise. Dullness settles in sealed rooms.

So much of staying alive inside—really alive—is about awareness. The dullness that creeps into old age isn't caused by time; it's caused by tuning out. When we stop noticing what's new, stop asking questions, and start assuming we've heard it all before, we begin to fade—not in body, but in spirit. The trick is to keep your antennae up. Listen more than you lecture, wonder more than you warn, and remember that the world is still unfolding, even if your own story feels well told. Life doesn't run out of things to show us; we just run out of interest if we're not careful.

The surest sign you're growing dull isn't your age—it's when people start avoiding you at morning tea. If your stories make others glance at the clock, it might be time for a little conversational spring-cleaning. The world doesn't stop being fascinating just because we've seen a lot of it; it's only boring if we stop paying attention. Ask questions. Laugh at things you don't understand. Be curious about the music, slang, and nonsense of the next generation—they'll love you for it. Growing old gracefully is fine, but growing old playfully is better.

The Last Laugh

Maybe growing old without growing dull is less about adding years and more about refusing to subtract personality. Life will shrink if we let it, but it will also expand if we keep saying, "Why not?"

There's a story of an 88-year-old woman who joined a university lecture on astronomy. When asked why, she said, "Because it's good to have something to look forward to — even if it's the stars."

That, surely, is the spirit we should all aim for: to keep looking up, even as gravity insists otherwise. A long life is wasted if you stop discovering.

Our Rule for Longevity #8:

Keep your stories short and your curiosity long.

Chapter 9

Casual Ageism

The Last Acceptable Prejudice

Old age is no place for sissies.

— Bette Davis

In a world obsessed with youth, ageing has become a quiet act of defiance. This chapter explores the subtle, systemic, and often well-intentioned disrespect that older adults face — in workplaces, hospitals, homes, and casual conversation — and reveals how those small daily dismissals add up to a global crisis of dignity. Yet beneath the statistics and stereotypes lies a more powerful truth: growing old is not decline, but achievement.

We've made progress in recognising racism, sexism, and other forms of discrimination, but ageism remains curiously acceptable—even fashionable. Anti-wrinkle ads fill our screens, 'anti-ageing' creams line our bathroom shelves, and social media glorifies youth as the only form of beauty worth pursuing. Growing older is treated like a moral failure, as though we've somehow neglected to stay young.

In workplaces, the experienced are quietly moved aside to make room for the 'dynamic'. In healthcare, symptoms are brushed off with, "What do you expect at your age?" In families, decisions are made for rather than with older relatives. And in popular culture, elders are either invisible or comic relief—sweet, confused, or quaintly 'tech-illiterate'.

The harm lies not just in the stereotypes, but in the erosion of dignity. When society stops listening to its elders, it loses a vital source of perspective, history, and calm—a compass forged by decades of trial and error.

The Quiet Disrespect of the Elderly

Ageism doesn't always shout. More often, it whispers. It slips into everyday language, into the sigh of impatience at a checkout, into the assumption that grey hair means frailty, confusion, or irrelevance. It hides beneath words like dear, sweetie, and still driving? Phrases that pretend warmth but often drip with condescension.

Evita: I remember so clearly the very first instance of casual ageism directed at me. I was barely sixty, which now seems relatively young. I was still working full-time. I thought I looked pretty good and youthful for sixty.

But in the eyes of this young, literal offender, I was simply an old woman.

I had been taking my relatively new car to the dealership for a service. The young man checking it in asked what the vehicle's odometer reading was.

When I told him that the current mileage was at 100,000, he remarked, "Ooh, you've done a lot of miles!"

At first the assumption surprised me. A lot of miles for who?

Smiling politely, I shot back, "Well, I do drive it every day, not just to church on Sundays".

Everyday Acts of Resistance

I mentioned the comment in my diplomatic response to the inevitable post-service "How Did We Do" survey from the vehicle manufacturer. I knew the young man hadn't meant to be casually ageist and I didn't want him to be reprimanded, but I did want to draw awareness to instances of casual, subconscious ageism, just as I would have to racism, sexism or misogyny.

I'm not a complainer and I would abhor being considered a 'Karen' – today's label for the stereotypically difficult middle-aged woman who is always demanding to see the manager – unfair to all the lovelies out there named Karen, a popular girls' name in the 1960s, 70s and 80s.

In any case, I didn't hear from the dealership, nor the manufacturer. It seems in asking for customer opinion they only wanted to hear the positive things.

For subsequent services, I took the car elsewhere.

Perceptions of Age

We've all done it, made assumptions not just about the elderly, but anyone older than us, without thinking that we'll be in that position too one day, if we're lucky. The alternative doesn't bear thinking about.

Evita: when our beloved grandmother died, she was only 60. Lionel and I were young children at the time. We thought Nana was as ancient as the Pyramids.

Old age – 60 – was a long way off for us.

Lionel: It still is, just in the other direction! But seriously, as we get older, we naturally push up our definition of old age. I now consider 'elderly' anything above 110 years of age!

The Subtle Act of Dismissal

If you're younger than us, use empathy to put yourself in our position and realise how irritating casual ageism can be.

Consider Natalie, a 79-year-old retired teacher who attends her grand-daughter's parent–teacher interview. The young teacher—kind, bright, and well-intentioned—speaks to her as if English were her second language. "That's wonderful, isn't it?" she says slowly, patting Natalie's hand. Natalie smiles politely but walks away feeling smaller than she did when she entered.

Or Natalie's sister, Susan, who at 85 recently moved into residential care due to physical constraints. On a daily basis, Susan tolerates the well-meaning but condescending attitudes of the carers, addressing the residents as though they're kindergarteners. "Come on now, we wouldn't want you to fall over, would we?" or speaking in loud commands, as though everyone is deaf.

Or take Kevin, now in his mid-90s, who still drives to the local shops. Each time he parks, someone comments, "Good on you for still being out and about!"—as if his independence were an act of defiance rather than the normal continuation of life. What's intended as a compliment lands instead as surprise: You're still functioning? Remarkable.

The Workplace Wall: Working over 60

Despite the likelihood for many of making it to 100 these days – and having to support ourselves financially in the meantime - trying to find work as a 60-year-old isn't easy. My daughter recently moved interstate and found herself constantly being passed over for employment positions, and not due to lack of qualification or experience.

Although one's age or date of birth doesn't have to be declared on a CV, college credentials dating back to the 1980s make it pretty apparent that the applicant is closing in on official retirement age.

A 2024 study by the University of Melbourne's Centre for Workplace Inclusion surveyed over 3,000 Australians aged 55 and older. Nearly 40% reported being turned down for jobs they were qualified for, with many citing subtle cues—phrases like "we're looking for a cultural fit" or "someone who can grow with the company."

One participant, a 62-year-old IT specialist, described applying for a role he'd practically written the manual for twenty years earlier. The recruiter never called back but later posted the position on LinkedIn with the tagline "ideal for a young tech gun." He said, "They didn't even realise how offensive that sounded. It's like they assumed I'd gone extinct."

This quiet exclusion is particularly cruel because it targets precisely those who have spent decades proving their worth. Experience becomes the very thing held against them.

Interpretation & Implications

These numbers show that older Australians are increasingly participating in work and society, yet structural and attitudinal barriers remain.

The fact that employers increasingly label people in their early 50s as 'older' suggests the threshold of 'acceptable age' is creeping downward.

The prevalence of self-reported discrimination signals that ageism is not just a perception, but a tangible experience for many.

The workforce shift means respecting and including older adults isn't optional—it's a social and economic imperative.

Disrespect beyond the workplace

Language matters: the small ways we speak to and about older adults shape how society values them — and how they value themselves.

Our friend, Ella, aged 78, enters the small hometown café where she used to bring her grandchildren after school. The barista greets her cheerfully: "Good morning, dear! Want me to pick something light for you?" Ella smiles and says, "Yes, one flat-white, please."

As she waits at the counter, a younger woman and her partner walk in behind her. The partner nods at Ella and says: "How lovely, hey — getting out and about at your age." Ella holds her steaming cup and hides a flicker of irritation. My age? she thinks. I'm still here, still active — why is that remarkable?

She finds a table and opens the newspaper. A broadband salesman at the next table leans over, sees her reading the tech section and says: "You must be pretty good with computers for someone of your generation." Ella closes her paper. Inside, she's thinking: Why am I being praised for doing something that's normal for me?

When she leaves, she pauses by the counter and thanks the barista. The barista adds a softer tone: "Take care, and don't over-do it now!" Ella nods, "I won't."

Walking out into the sunshine, she reflects on how every friendly comment carried a hidden assumption: that age = less capability, less independence. She wonders: if she were thirty years younger, would anyone compliment her for being in a café at 8 a.m., reading a newspaper and paying for her flat-white? Probably not.

The café door closes behind her and she senses that the world still thinks of older people as a separate category — one deserving gentle praise for merely existing. And she realises: day by day, moment by moment, dignity can be eroded not by overt insult, but by the micro-expressions of surprise, condescension and lowered expectation.

Ageism in Healthcare

Consider this vignette. Our friend Audrey, 82, is admitted to a busy public hospital, following a fall at home. Her daughter, Clare, stays by her side, noticing how the staff interact with her mother. The nurses address Audrey with a tone that feels more patronizing than professional, often speaking over her to Clare, as if Audrey isn't present. When Audrey mentions a history of heart disease, the response is a dismissive nod and a quick change of subject.

One morning, a doctor enters and begins discussing Audrey's treatment plan with Clare, without acknowledging Audrey directly. Clare gently interrupts, saying, "Actually, Mom is the patient." The doctor pauses, then turns to Audrey, but the conversation remains brief and impersonal. Audrey feels invisible, her decades of life experience reduced to a mere statistic in a crowded ward.

Later, Clare overhears a nurse remarking, "She's had a good innings," implying that Audrey age somehow diminishes her worthiness of comprehensive care. The comment stings, highlighting the subtle yet pervasive ageism that permeates even the most professional settings.

Ageism in healthcare is a significant issue in developed countries, affecting the quality of care and treatment older adults receive. Recent studies and reports have highlighted the prevalence and impact of age-related discrimination in medical settings, finding that older adults often experience ageism in healthcare, with common instances including dismissive attitudes towards symptoms and assumptions about the inevitability of decline due to age.

Ageism has an impact on treatment, too, as attitudes can lead to older patients receiving substandard care. For example, medical professionals may attribute treatable conditions to normal aging, resulting in underdiagnosis or delayed treatment.

Legislation prohibits discrimination on the basis of age in various sectors, including healthcare. However, enforcement and awareness remain challenges, and many older individuals are unaware of their rights or feel powerless to assert them.

Calls for Reform

Advocacy groups are urging for systemic changes to address ageism in healthcare. This includes training for healthcare professionals to recognize and combat ageist biases, as well as policies that ensure equitable treatment for older patients.

Addressing ageism in healthcare is crucial for ensuring that older citizens receive the respect and quality care they deserve. Recognizing and confronting these biases is the first step toward creating a more inclusive and equitable healthcare system for all ages.

The Emotional Toll

Ageism chips away at confidence. When society repeatedly tells older people that they're slowing down, they begin to believe it. A lifetime of self-sufficiency can unravel under the constant drizzle of diminishment—like water eroding stone.

Psychologists now recognise "internalised ageism" as a real and damaging phenomenon. Those who absorb society's negative messages about ageing are more likely to experience depression, social withdrawal, and even cognitive decline. The body follows where the mind leads.

A Global Condition

This quiet prejudice isn't confined to any one nation. The World Health Organization (WHO) calls ageism a global epidemic — the most widespread and socially accepted forms of discrimination on the planet. Roughly one in two people worldwide hold moderate to high ageist attitudes. That means roughly half of humanity carries some form of bias against its older members; its own future selves. A quiet, almost invisible prejudice woven into speech, systems, and policy.

This is not just about unkind jokes or dismissive tones; ageism has measurable, damaging consequences. The consequences are tangible. Across 45 countries and more than seven million participants, a comprehensive global review found that in over 95% of studies, ageism was linked to worse physical or mental health outcomes. Those who internalised society's negative views about ageing were more likely to experience depression, cognitive decline, heart disease, and even shorter lifespans. In other words, ageism doesn't just wound pride — it literally shortens lives.

In healthcare, the bias is especially damaging. A European systematic review found that in 85 percent of medical studies, age influenced who received certain treatments or procedures. Older patients were more likely to be denied surgery or advanced therapies, not because of medical unsuitability, but because of assumptions about futility or cost. This is discrimination dressed up as pragmatism.

A survey across Europe found that one in three older adults reported experiencing ageism directly — through insults, exclusion, or denial of services based purely on age. These are not isolated acts of rudeness but patterns of structural bias, the kind that shape hospital policies, insurance limits, and social attitudes alike.

The consequences extend beyond the human toll to the economic. In the United States, researchers calculated that negative age stereotypes and self-perceptions among those over 60 added an excess annual cost of US $63 billion to the healthcare system. Ageism, it seems, is not just morally corrosive — it's fiscally foolish. The same logic applies globally: every time older people are marginalised or written off, societies lose their contributions, their taxes, their care work, and their hard-won experience.

Despite the scope of the problem, the WHO notes that data from low- and middle-income countries remains sparse. We know that elders are well respected and age revered in some cultures, but we know little about how ageism manifests in other regions — a silence that speaks volumes. The absence of data does not mean the absence of discrimination; more often, it signals that those affected have not been heard

Everywhere you look, the story repeats: many cultures celebrate youth but fear their own aging process. Ageism wears different masks — politeness in one place, efficiency in another — but beneath them all lies the same misunderstanding: that the old are somehow "other."

It is as present in hospital corridors as in corporate boardrooms. The world is growing older — by 2050, one in six people will be over 65 — yet our attitudes toward ageing have not kept pace with our demographics.

If half the world still quietly believes that to age is to diminish, then the work ahead is not merely social or political; it is moral. The global statistics are a mirror, and what they reflect is simple but confronting:

we cannot claim to value longevity while demeaning those who embody it.

Relearning Respect

Respect is not nostalgia. It's not about treating the elderly as relics of a better time. It's about recognising their ongoing humanity—seeing them not as past tense but as present.

Cultures that revere elders aren't sentimental; they're pragmatic. They understand that longevity brings perspective. In Japan, the word ikigai captures the idea of having a reason for being—something many older Japanese continue to nurture well into their 90s, with society's full support. In contrast, Western societies often treat retirement as an ending rather than a transformation.

Imagine if instead of asking, "When will you slow down?" we asked, "What do you want to explore next?" If instead of calling someone "adorable" for remembering their PIN number, we asked for their opinion on interest rates, city planning, or politics. Imagine the cultural shift if wisdom were seen not as quaint but as currency.

Combating ageism doesn't require legislation—though workplace protections help. It starts in the micro-moments.

Respect, not reverence, is what elders want — to be seen, heard, and consulted, not coddled or sidelined.

Our advice for those working or dealing with elders:

- **Speak directly, not down.** Avoid the sing-song tone that would insult a five-year-old.

- **Challenge stereotypes.** When someone says, "Old people can't use technology," point out your grandmother who manages her share portfolio on her iPad.

- **Include, don't exclude.** Don't assume an older person wouldn't enjoy a concert, a road trip, or a tech gadget. Ask. Invite. Include.

- **Use names, not endearments or nicknames.** Call people by who they are, not what you assume them to be.

Every act of genuine respect pushes back against a culture that too easily forgets its elders.

Growing Older Without Shrinking

Ageing is not a disease, and old age is not a problem to be solved. It is an achievement—a long, improbable victory over the odds. Each wrinkle is a chapter, each year a testament. The goal is not to be treated like you're still young, but to be treated as if you still matter.

In the end, ageism is a failure of imagination. It reflects a society that can picture youth but not wisdom, that values speed over substance, and novelty over depth. To grow old without growing dull requires a culture brave enough to see beyond the surface.

And that begins with one simple truth: respect should not have an expiry date.

Reclaiming Age as an Achievement

To grow old is to win — not by luck, but by endurance, adaptability, and the quiet art of survival. Yet somewhere along the way, we stopped seeing age as an accomplishment and began treating it as an inconvenience. We celebrate youth for its promise and middle age for its productivity, but the old are expected to retreat politely into the background.

This shrinking of status is not inevitable. It is a choice society makes — and one it can unmake. Reclaiming age as an achievement means more than asking for courtesy; it means reshaping the story. Instead of being spoken to, older people must be invited to speak with. Instead of pity, curiosity. Instead of surprise at competence, respect for continuity.

We must stop treating elders as though they are passengers on the slow train to irrelevance. They are the living archives of everything we've learned — the keepers of perspective in an impatient world. Every older person you meet has survived more change than most of us can imagine, and still finds a way to laugh, to love, to adapt.

In truth, ageism is a failure of imagination — the inability to picture oneself a few decades down the road — and a failure of gratitude. Every elder is proof of what's possible: that life can continue, deepen, and matter long after youth fades.

Growing old is not a tragedy. It is the only way to live long enough to understand what life was really about. The task, then, is not to deny age but to dignify it — to remind the world that respect should never have an expiry date.

Growing older with dignity isn't just about resisting ageism — it's about cultivating the kind of emotional strength that laughter, forgiveness, and lightness make possible. And that's where we turn next: to the quiet superpower of the emotional immune system — the art of laughing and letting go.

Our Rule for Longevity #9

Never Apologise for Your Age.

The moment you start apologising for your age, you begin to shrink into the space others make for you. Don't. You've earned every year — every wrinkle, lesson, and scar. Wear them as evidence of survival, not decline. The world may overlook the old, but longevity thrives in those who refuse to disappear. Confidence, not compliance, is the true fountain of youth.

Chapter 10

Don't Be a Judge

NOR A PEARL-CLUTCHER

It is not how old you are, but how you are old.

– Jules Renard

Some people clutch pearls at the sight of a tattoo, a nose ring, or neon hair and act as if the world is falling apart. Newsflash: it's not. The world is fine—brighter, bolder, and more interesting than ever. The only thing in danger is your sense of humor if you don't learn to mind your own business.

There's a peculiar pastime some older people seem to enjoy: judging the younger generations. It can manifest in many forms, but one of the most visible is the commentary on appearance. Raised eyebrows, a nudge, whispered disapproval, or outright condemnation.

Muttered comments about "in my day" are all too common. Tattoos, piercings, colorful hair—suddenly, these personal choices are treated like crimes.

Remember that personal appearance is just that—personal. What someone chooses to put on their skin, in their hair, or on their face is a form of self-expression, a story, a celebration of who they are. It's as legitimate as the choices *you* make: the clothes you wear, the car you drive, or the music that moves you. Judging these choices says far more about the judge than the judged.

Evita: My former friend, Jan, was always very opinionated, which is fine - when opinions are being sought. But she seemed to feel as though only her opinion counted, and she was openly and audibly judgmental about strangers to the point of embarrassment.

Once, during a hospital stay, she openly berated a young dietitian about his weight. "I'm surprised anyone working in healthcare, let alone specialise in nutrition, could let themselves get so fat!" she snorted.

The poor young man explained that he had a genetic hormonal irregularity that contributed to his weight. That is precisely what led him to a career in dietetics, so he could help others facing the same issues. That put Jan in her place.

Evita continues: If we were at the supermarket, Jan would openly display her horror towards the overweight, the tattooed, pierced, barefoot; the list was endless. I would try to shush her, remind her of her rebellious years, or quietly explain that people could do whatever they wanted to their own bodies.

Jan was the epitome of the horrified pearl-clutcher, loudly tut-tutting and voicing her disapproval in a loud whisper.

"They *want* to be looked at!" was her defense.

"Not necessarily," I protested. "They just want to be able to express themselves".

I was too fed up, ashamed of her behaviour and her closed-mindedness. Even my children, as toddlers, had known better than to point out anyone different.

So, I added something bold, for perspective:

"Do you think that young lass approves of those superflous hairs on your chin? Or maybe she thinks you keep them there for attention".

Needless to say, we'd definitely reached the point at which we could no longer remain in each other's company, and the last I saw Jan, she was nervously fingering her chin for the offending hairs.

Lionel: I've had similar experiences with my peers. I met up with my friend, Bob, 90, for coffee one morning. Bob squinted at Emma, the new young barista who had a shaved head and tattooed forearms. To my humiliation he wrinkled his nose, whispering loudly, "Why would anyone do that to themselves?"

Emma couldn't help but hear and as she delivered our perfect coffees to the table, explained that she had shaved off her hair in solidarity with her sister who was going through chemotherapy, and that the tattoos were to honour her grandfathers and uncles who had died in military service.

While Emma didn't need to justify her decisions, she had patiently put Bob in his place and taught him a hard lesson about keeping his opinions to himself.

One never knows what others are going through and we need to think before we speak.

Judging the choices of others doesn't reveal anything about the person being judged. It only exposes the judge's discomfort with change, or sometimes, a longing for a past that never really existed.

Remember, You Rebelled Once

Older generations often forget—or choose to forget—that they once pushed the boundaries themselves. The mini-skirts of the 1960s, the long hair of the 1970s, the mohawks and safety pins of the 1980s—they all once scandalized the previous generation. Yet today, those same trends are occasionally revered as nostalgia, proof of cultural significance, or "classics." The double standard is glaring.

Pearl-clutching criticism is not just harmless chatter; it can make people feel marginalized or unwelcome in the world they are trying to navigate. Respecting others' choices doesn't mean you have to understand them. It doesn't require agreement or imitation. It means simply acknowledging that every person has the right to present themselves as they wish, without fear of ridicule.

The world grows richer, more vibrant, and more inclusive when diversity of expression is welcomed rather than criticized. The next time you feel the impulse to clutch pearls at a tattoo sleeve or gasp at a septum piercing, pause. Ask yourself: does your judgment contribute to understanding, or does it only feed your own nostalgia and discomfort? Often, the wisest response is silence—or better yet, curiosity. Think about the appropriateness of asking about the story behind the ink, the reason for the piercing, or the meaning of the hair color. You might just learn something—and you might also learn to appreciate the freedom of letting people be themselves.

The world grows richer, more vibrant, and more inclusive when diversity of expression is welcomed rather than criticized.

Because life is too short—and too rich in experiences—to waste on judging how someone chooses to live it. The world is more fun when we admire the color instead of wasting energy being horrified.

Stop Judging: Life's Too Bright for Sepia Tones

So, let's make a deal: before you gasp at a neon hair streak, or a sleeve of tattoos, take a breath. Remember that everyone is simply trying to navigate life in their own colorful way. Your judgment won't change their choices—but your respect just might make the world a little kinder, a little brighter, and a lot more interesting. After all, if life were only about staying inside the lines, it would be terribly dull. And we'd all be wearing beige.

A person with a tattoo or an unconventional hairstyle isn't asking for approval—they are asserting their identity, exploring their creativity, and, in many cases, simply enjoying the process of being themselves. Condemnation in these moments is unnecessary, and worse, it perpetuates a culture of judgment that narrows the human experience.

Respecting others' choices doesn't mean you have to understand them. It doesn't require agreement or imitation. It means simply acknowledging that every person has the right to present themselves as they wish, without fear of ridicule. The world grows richer, more vibrant, and more inclusive when diversity of expression is welcomed rather than criticized.

So, the next time you feel the impulse to clutch pearls at a neck tattoo or gasp at a nose ring, pause. Ask yourself: does your judgment contribute to understanding, or does it only feed your own nostalgia and discomfort? Often, the wisest response is silence—or better yet, curiosity. Ask about the story behind the ink, the reason for the piercing, or the meaning of the hair color. You might just learn something—and you might also learn to appreciate the freedom of letting people be themselves.

Because life is too short—and too rich in experiences—to waste on judging how someone chooses to live it. Tattoos fade, piercings close, and hair grows out—but judgment leaves a wrinkle in your soul.

Always remember:

- **Personal expression—tattoos, piercings, hair color—is a form of identity. Respect it.**

- **Judging others says more about you than the person you're judging.**

- **Curiosity beats criticism: ask about the story, don't assume the meaning.**

- **Everyone has the right to live their life in color—let them.**

- **Don't waste energy on disapproval. Embrace the vibrancy around you.**

Our Rule for Longevity #10:

Judge not, lest ye be judged. Respect everyone's journey, even if it looks nothing like your own.

Chapter 11

Laughing and Letting Go

The Emotional Immune System

How old would you be if you didn't know how old you were?

– Satchel Paige

Over the years we've noticed that the people who live longest aren't always the fittest or the wealthiest. They're the ones who bounce back from life's little humiliations. The ones who trip, curse, laugh, and keep walking.

Evita: They say laughter is the best medicine. I wouldn't go that far — antibiotics still have the edge — but laughter certainly comes with fewer side effects.

We call it the emotional immune system — that quiet, internal strength that stops life's irritations from turning into infections.

Much like our physical immune system protects us from illness, we've discovered that our emotional resilience shields us from life's inevitable storms. After decades of weathering losses, changes, and challenges, we've learned that emotional well-being isn't just about feeling good - it's about building an internal fortress that helps us bounce back from adversity. Like the intertwining branches of a vine offering strength and support, our emotional well-being acts as an invisible shield, protecting both mind and body through life's inevitable storms.

After watching countless peers struggle with the weight of un-processed emotions, we've learned that emotional resilience isn't something you're born with - it's a skill you cultivate, like tending a garden. And just like a garden, it needs daily attention, gentle pruning, and room to grow.

What medical science is only beginning to understand, we've wit-nessed firsthand: how laughter lightens the load on your heart, how forgiveness eases the ache in your joints, how gratitude strengthens your immune system as surely as any vitamin.

These aren't just metaphors. The connection between emotional and physical health becomes clearer with each passing decade. We've watched friends who carried grudges age faster than those who learned to let go. We've seen how bitterness can bend a spine more surely than osteoporosis.

Over our lives, we've developed what we call an 'emotional immune system' - not to avoid feeling, but to process feelings in ways that heal rather than harm. It's about building resilience without becoming hard, staying sensitive without becoming fragile.

This chapter explores how to strengthen your emotional immune system - not through strict rules or complicated practices, but through small, daily choices that add up to a lifetime of emotional health. Because the longest-lived people we've known weren't just physically healthy - they were emotionally resilient.

We'll share what we've learned about letting go, laughing often, and loving anyway - even after loss. Most importantly, we'll explore how to keep your heart both strong and soft as the years unfold. Because that balance, we've found, is the true secret to living not just longer, but more fully.

Building Emotional Resilience Through Gratitude

Gratitude, we've discovered, is like a muscle in the emotional immune system - the more you exercise it, the stronger it becomes. After decades of witnessing both hardship and joy, we've learned that cultivating gratitude isn't just about saying "thank you" - it's about training your heart to find light even in life's shadows.

Evita: I remember clearly the day this truth crystallized for me. I was sitting in the garden, feeling the weight of my husband's absence, when a small brown bird landed nearby. It was nothing special - just an ordinary sparrow - but watching it hop about, so present in its simple existence, something shifted in me.

I was grateful for that small moment of connection with life itself. Something in me lifted that day. The conventional wisdom said to 'stay strong' and 'keep busy.' But it was only when I allowed myself to feel fully - to cry, to remember, to laugh at old memories - that the pressure began to ease.

Lionel: And I learned through forgiveness. For years, I carried resentment toward an old business partner who had betrayed my trust. That anger sat in my stomach like a stone, affecting my appetite, my sleep, my outlook. The day I finally let it go, my whole body felt lighter.

This practice of noticing and appreciating small moments has become our daily medicine. Not the forced gratitude of social media posts or greeting cards, but the quiet recognition of life's continuing gifts: morning light through curtains, the warmth of a cup of tea, a phone call from a grandchild.

Science now confirms what we've learned through experience - that gratitude actually changes the brain's chemistry, strengthening emotional resilience and reducing stress. Research shows that people who maintain grateful perspectives cope better with adversity and experience better mental health outcomes.

Lionel: I've made it a habit to start each day by naming three things I'm grateful for, before my feet even touch the floor. Sometimes they're profound things - health, family, news of a signed international peace deal. Other times they're delightfully ordinary - the comfort of my pillow, the sound of rain, the prospect of breakfast. This simple practice has transformed how I meet each day.

We've noticed that grateful people tend to age more gracefully. They complain less, laugh more, and seem to weather life's storms with greater resilience. It's not that they don't face difficulties - we all do - but they've developed the ability to hold both challenge and appreciation in the same heart.

Here's what we've learned about building emotional resilience through gratitude:

- **Start small.** Notice the ordinary pleasures: a hot shower, a comfortable chair, a moment of quiet.

- **Make it a ritual.** Whether morning or evening, set aside time to acknowledge what's good.

- **Share your gratitude.** Tell people what you appreciate about them while you can.

- **Use gratitude to reframe challenges.** Ask "What can I learn from this?" or "What remains to be thankful for?"

- **Keep a gratitude journal,** even if it's just in your head.

Remember, the importance of companionship in managing stress cannot be emphasised enough.

The practice of gratitude doesn't deny life's difficulties - it simply reminds us that difficulty isn't the whole story. Even in our darkest moments, there are threads of light to be found if we train ourselves to look for them.

Evita: Recently, when I was struggling with a health setback, I started listing everything that still worked well in my body - my eyes that could still read, my hands that could still hold a cup, my heart that kept beating without any conscious effort on my part. This simple practice shifted my focus from what I'd lost to what remained.

Gratitude, we've found, is both a shield and a compass - it protects us from despair while pointing us toward what truly matters. In our ninth decade, we've learned that a grateful heart is a resilient one, capable of finding joy even in life's winter seasons.

Managing Stress and Anxiety in Later Years

Managing stress and anxiety becomes more crucial - and sometimes more challenging - as the decades accumulate. We've watched countless friends and family members struggle with worry, and we've developed our own quiet wisdom about keeping the mind steady when life feels turbulent.

Evita: I remember clearly the moment I truly understood the connection between emotional and physical health. It was during a particularly stressful period when several friends had passed away in quick succession. My blood pressure had risen, my sleep was poor, and my appetite had vanished. Then one afternoon, while sitting with my sister-in-law who was sharing similar concerns, we spontaneously began reminiscing about old times, laughing at long-forgotten stories. By the end of that afternoon, I felt physically lighter. My shoulders had relaxed, my breathing had deepened, and even my appetite had returned.

Lionel: Yes, and I've noticed how those who maintain their sense of humor tend to weather life's storms better, like the Tipton twins' famous quip about "no sex and plenty of Guinness". How I wish I'd thought of that! Things like that do more than just make people smile – they show how humor can lift us above our circumstances.

When reflecting recently, we developed what we call our 'emotional immune system' - a set of habits and attitudes that help us bounce back from stress and anxiety. Like our physical immune system, it needs daily care and attention.

Here's what we've learned works best:

- **Start each day with gratitude.** Before the worries rush in, name three simple things you're thankful for.

- **Use laughter as medicine.** Watch something funny, share jokes, find humor in small absurdities.

- **Keep connected but choose your company wisely.** Some people calm us; others stir up anxiety.

- **Create quiet moments.** The world moves too fast - slow down, breathe, watch the birds.

- **Let go of what you can't control.** Energy spent worrying is energy wasted.

We've noticed that anxiety often comes from trying to control too much. The more we can accept change and uncertainty as natural parts of life, the lighter our mental load becomes. This doesn't mean giving up or giving in - it means choosing our battles wisely.

Evita: When I feel anxiety rising, I use what I call my 'five breath reset.' I stop whatever I'm doing and take five slow, deep breaths. With the first breath, I acknowledge what's troubling me. With the second, I ask myself if there's anything useful I can do about it right now. With the third, I either take action or consciously let it go. It's simple, but it works. By the fifth, I'm ready to resume, with renewed calmness.

Lionel: And I've learned to treat stress like weather - it comes, it goes, and fighting it only makes it worse. Instead of resisting anxious feelings, I observe them with curiosity. This slight shift in perspective often helps them pass more quickly.

Research confirms what we've learned through experience - that emotional resilience is linked to better physical health and increased longevity. The ability to adapt, recover, and even thrive in the face of stress isn't just about feeling better - it's about living longer and more fully.

Our advice? Build your emotional immune system as carefully as you would care for your physical health. Laugh often, love freely, let go regularly, and remember that every storm eventually passes. Your heart and your health will thank you for it.

Connecting Emotional Health and Longevity

The connection between emotional well-being and physical longevity isn't just folk wisdom - it's supported by decades of scientific research. We've witnessed this truth firsthand through nine decades of observing our friends and family, noticing how those who maintain emotional balance tend to live longer, healthier lives.

Evita: I remember watching my dear friend Shirl who, despite facing numerous health challenges, maintained an unwavering positive outlook. Her doctors were consistently amazed by her resilience and recovery rates. Years later, research would confirm what we observed - that optimistic individuals are indeed more likely to reach age 85 or older and experience better health outcomes.

Science now validates what we've long suspected - that our emotional state profoundly impacts our physical health. Studies show that chronic stress, anxiety, and negative emotions can trigger sustained activation of the autonomic nervous system, raising blood pressure and suppressing immune function. Conversely, positive emotions and relaxation techniques have been proven to improve immune response and reduce disease risk.

Lionel: The mind-body connection becomes more apparent with each passing year. I've noticed how my own stress levels directly affect my physical well-being. When I'm worried or upset, my joints ache more, my digestion suffers, and my sleep becomes disturbed. Learning to manage these emotional states has become as important as any medication.

Here's what we've learned about nurturing emotional health for longevity:

- **Practice daily gratitude** - it's not just good for the spirit, it's good for the body.

- **Maintain strong social connections** - they're as vital as any vitamin.

- **Develop stress management techniques** that work for you.

- **Allow yourself to experience and process emotions** rather than suppressing them.

- **Keep your sense of humor** - laughter truly is powerful medicine.

The Harvard Optimism Study confirms what we've observed - individuals with higher optimism show better physical functioning and lower incidence of chronic diseases in later life. It's not about denying life's challenges, but rather about developing resilience in facing them.

Evita: I've made it a practice to start each day with what I call my 'emotional vitamin' - a moment of quiet gratitude, followed by connection with someone I care about, even if it's just a brief phone call. These simple practices have become as crucial to my well-being as any physical exercise.

Lionel: And I've learned that emotional resilience isn't about avoiding negative feelings - it's about developing the capacity to bounce back from them. Like a muscle, this resilience grows stronger with use. Each challenge we face and overcome adds to our emotional immune system.

The evidence is clear - nurturing emotional health isn't just about feeling good, it's about living longer and better. Studies across populations confirm that social connection and positive emotional states are universal predictors of improved health and reduced risk of early death.

Through decades of watching, living, and learning, we've discovered that emotional well-being isn't just about feeling good - it's about creating an internal environment where both body and spirit can thrive. Like a well-tended garden, our emotional health requires daily attention, gentle pruning, and room to grow.

We've watched countless friends succeed or struggle based not on their physical strength, but on their emotional resilience. Those who learned to laugh easily, forgive readily, and adapt gracefully seemed to weather life's storms with remarkable strength. Those who held onto bitterness or refused to process grief often aged faster, regardless of their physical care.

Evita: The other day, my granddaughter asked me what I considered the most important 'vitamin' for longevity. I told her, "Laughter - taken daily, shared often, and never rationed." She thought I was joking, but I've never been more serious. A light heart keeps the body buoyant.

Lionel: And I've learned that emotional resilience isn't about avoiding feelings - it's about moving through them with grace. Like physical exercise, emotional wellness requires both exertion and recovery. We must feel fully, release completely, and keep our hearts supple through regular use.

As we close this chapter on emotional health, remember that your emotional immune system needs the same careful attention as your physical one. Cultivate gratitude like you would tend a garden. Practice forgiveness as regularly as you take your morning walk. Let laughter be your daily medicine.

Most importantly, remember that emotional resilience isn't about being unshakeable - it's about learning to bend instead of break, to flow instead of fight, to rise again after every fall.

Because in the end, what keeps us young isn't the strength of our muscles, but the resilience of our spirits.

The Chemistry of Cheerfulness

Lionel: When I turned ninety, my doctor said, "Congratulations."

I said, "For what — showing up?"

He laughed and said, "For staying alive."

Fair enough. Then he asked what I'd learned.

I told him: Longevity isn't the prize. It's the opportunity. The longer you live, the more chances you get to get things right — or at least funnier.

Scientists say laughter releases endorphins. We say it releases people.

You can't laugh and stay tense at the same time. Laughing is a reset button for the soul. A small act of rebellion against gloom. I've laughed at funerals, at doctor's appointments, at my own misfortunes — not because they were funny, but because humour keeps despair from moving in permanently.

Beware of being 'toxically positive', though. Sometimes all we need is a good mope, a whine (or wine) and chocolate. Gratitude doesn't have to be saccharine — just a steady, grounded appreciation for having made it this far.

Letting Go of the Grudge Collection

Train your emotional immune system. Laugh often, forgive freely, and don't take the bait of bitterness. The heart, like the body, grows stronger through recovery, not resistance.

Holding grudges, we've learned, is like drinking old milk — it only curdles you. People sometimes ask if I've forgiven everyone who's wronged me. Not quite. But I've stopped rehearsing their crimes.

When you let go, you reclaim energy you didn't know you were wasting. It's like finally deleting old emails — the relief is immediate.

Evita: A dear childhood friend, Jo, and I fell out in our twenties, over her then-boyfriend who, it turned out, didn't last very long.

Even so, we missed out on decades of each other's' lives until one day, Jo and I reconnected through the newly discovered thing called social media.

We still share laughter about the 'missing years', the loser boyfriend and the absurdity of the past.

The Art of Forgetting

If there's an art to remembering, there's also an art to forgetting — and it might be just as important to a long, peaceful life. We may keep their memories sharp, but we also know how to let the small stuff slide. The trick, it seems, isn't to remember everything, but to remember well.

We tend to treat memory like a trophy cabinet: the more we keep, the better. Yet a good memory isn't everything. The human mind is more like a well-run wardrobe — it works best when we clear out what no longer fits. Forgetting, done gracefully, makes space for living

Evita: Some things are best remembered vaguely — especially where we put the chocolates.

The Brain's Spring Cleaning

Neuroscientists now know that forgetting is not a failure but a feature. The brain actively prunes old information through a process called synaptic remodeling. While we sleep, neural connections are quietly rearranged; what's essential is reinforced, and what's irrelevant fades. It's mental housekeeping — and without it, the attic of our minds would collapse under the weight of trivia.

The psychologist Oliver Hardt calls it 'adaptive forgetting' — the ability to discard outdated knowledge so we can focus on what still matters.

His study proposes that forgetting is an active and well-regulated process, essential for efficient memory function. It challenges the traditional view of forgetting as a passive decay, highlighting its role in memory organization and prioritization.

In other words, forgetting helps us stay present. Imagine if you vividly recalled every phone number you've ever dialled, every parking ticket you've ever paid. You'd be paralysed by memory.

What We Choose to Forget

Healthy forgetting is often emotional. We let go of grudges, humiliations, and regrets — the brain's equivalent of decluttering the junk drawer. Those who hold on too tightly to past injuries often show higher levels of stress hormones and inflammation. Letting go isn't denial; it's maintenance.

An old friend of mine, Harold, put it best. At ninety-two, he was asked how he managed to stay cheerful despite a string of family squabbles over the years. "Easy," he said. "Selective amnesia. I just forget what people owe me and remember what they bring."

That's the art of forgetting: a deliberate, generous blindness to the unhelpful.

Maybe that's what real longevity looks like: not a mind bursting with everything it's seen, but one at ease with what it no longer needs to remember. The years that slip away aren't losses; they're quiet acts of editing — and a well-edited life reads better than a cluttered one.

The Wisdom of Letting Go

Evita: I tried the new decluttering craze once. Turns out, it's not the objects that need sorting — it's the attachment.

Lionel: Letting go used to sound like defeat. Now it feels like relief.

Emotional longevity — that inner steadiness we've spoken of — depends as much on release as on recall. Those who dwell constantly on what went wrong, or who replay every loss, tire themselves out. Meanwhile, those who can say, "Ah well, that was then," seem to carry less weight on their backs and fewer furrows on their brows.

A good life, like a good garden, thrives on pruning. You don't mourn every weed you pull — you make room for what's still growing.

Vignette: The Piano Teacher

Alan, seventy-eight, once taught piano to children. When arthritis crept into his hands, he stopped playing — but not teaching. He jokes that his fingers retired before he did.

"I used to mourn what I'd lost," he said, "but then I realised my students had taken it with them. Every scale they play keeps a bit of me alive. So I've decided to forget the loss and remember the echo."

His ability to let go of what he can no longer do — without resentment, without self-pity — is its own kind of mastery. It's the kind of forgetting that enlarges life rather than shrinking it.

The Practical Side

So, how do we practise the art of forgetting?

- **Sleep well.** Memory consolidation and memory clearing both happen while we rest.

- **Forgive quickly.** Not for others, but for the peace it brings your own circuitry.

- **Avoid rumination.** Re-reading old emotional mail serves no purpose. Delete it.

- **Live forward.** Keep learning, keep moving, keep planning. The brain prioritises what it expects to use.

- **Don't sweat – or try to remember – the small stuff.**

- **Cultivate your emotional immune system as carefully as your physical one.** Laugh often, love freely, let go regularly - your heart and your health will thank you for it.

Our final advice? Treat your emotional well-being as seriously as you do your physical health. Build and maintain meaningful relationships. Practice forgiveness - not just of others, but of yourself. Find reasons to laugh every day. These aren't just nice ideas - they're survival strategies backed by both science and experience.

Because in the end, a long life isn't just about the strength of your body - it's about the resilience of your spirit.At the close of this chapter on emotional resilience and longevity, we're reminded that our internal fortress - built of laughter, forgiveness, and gratitude - may be our strongest shield against time itself.

Our Rule for Longevity #11

Travel lighter as you go. What you release makes room for what's real.

Chapter 12

Resilience

Accepting Change and Mortality

The afternoon knows what the morning never suspected.

— Robert Frost

At ninety-five, we've come to understand that accepting mortality isn't about surrendering to it, but rather about embracing the precious nature of each moment we're given. Like watching the seasons change, there's a quiet beauty in understanding that every phase of life, including its eventual conclusion, has its own purpose and dignity. Like watching the seasons change in our garden, accepting life's transitions has become second nature after ninety-five years. The body may protest, but the spirit grows more supple with each passing season.

When you reach our age, you've had a lifetime of holding on — to people, to dreams, to memories, even grudges. You discover that peace comes not from clinging, but from loosening your grip on what was and embracing what is.

Letting go isn't giving up — it's giving over to the natural flow of life. It's understanding that strength often lies in flexibility rather than resistance. Just as a reed bends in the storm while the rigid oak might break, we've learned that resilience comes from adapting rather than fighting against change.

Evita: After decades of watching friends and family members struggle against the inevitable changes that come with aging, I've come to see acceptance as a form of grace. Those who fight against every wrinkle, who deny every limitation, often seem to age faster than those who greet each change with curiosity and adaptation.

Lionel: The art of aging well, we've discovered, isn't about maintaining everything exactly as it was — it's about finding new ways to flourish within each phase of life. Like our garden, which changes with each season yet remains vibrant in its own way, we too must learn to bloom differently as time passes.

This chapter explores how we've learned to navigate these changes while maintaining our dignity and sense of self. We'll share our experiences with physical limitations, shifting roles, and yes, even mortality itself. Because understanding how to accept change without being diminished by it might be the most important skill we've developed in our ninety-plus years.

Most importantly, we'll discuss how making peace with mortality has actually helped us live more fully. When you stop running from the inevitable, you gain the freedom to focus on what truly matters — the relationships, the moments of joy, the simple pleasures that make each day worth living.

Through personal stories, practical wisdom, and the lessons we've gathered over nearly a century of living, we'll explore how to maintain resilience while gracefully accepting life's natural progression. Because true longevity isn't just about adding years to life — it's about finding peace within each stage of the journey.

Making Peace with Physical Changes

Our bodies change. That's not news to anyone who's lived past forty, but at ninety-five, we've learned that physical changes aren't just inevitable - they're invitations to discover new ways of being.

Evita: I remember the morning I first noticed I couldn't reach the top shelf without a step stool. Instead of frustration, I felt a strange peace. My body was teaching me something about adaptation, about finding new ways to accomplish old tasks.

Lionel: And I recall when my knees started protesting against gardening. Rather than give up my beloved hobby, I discovered the joy of kneeling mats, raised beds and long-handled tools. The methods are different but the garden still blooms.

Making peace with physical changes isn't about surrender - it's about creativity and resilience. Like Verla Starkey and Merla Swenson, fellow nonagenarian twins we've read about, we've learned that adaptation is key. They found that living together helped them navigate physical changes through mutual support and shared laughter.

Here's what we've learned about making peace with our changing bodies:

- **Accept changes as natural transitions, not personal failures.**

- **Focus on what you can still do, not what you've lost.**

- **Find new ways to accomplish familiar tasks.**

- **Maintain movement within your current abilities.**

- **Keep your sense of humor about physical changes.**

The body's transformations are universal - decreased muscle mass, reduced skin elasticity, slower mobility, and sensory changes. But how we respond to these changes shapes our experience of aging far more than the changes themselves.

We've discovered that acceptance doesn't mean resignation. When our vision began to dim, we didn't stop reading - we got better lighting and larger print books. When our balance became less reliable, we didn't stop moving - we added handrails and practiced chair yoga.

We've learned to celebrate what our bodies can still do rather than mourn what they cannot.

The key is to maintain dignity while adapting to change. We've found that daily routines and small pleasures become even more important as our physical capabilities shift. A warm bath becomes not just cleansing but therapeutic. A gentle morning stretch routine becomes not just exercise but meditation.

Evita: Sometimes I catch my reflection and barely recognize myself. But then I smile, and there I am - still me, just in a more seasoned package.

These wrinkles and grey hairs have been earned through decades of laughter, worry, and wonder.

Lionel: And when my hands shake slightly while painting, I've learned to incorporate that tremor into my art. Some of my most interesting work has come from accepting these changes rather than fighting them.

Making peace with physical changes requires a delicate balance between acceptance and adaptation. It's about finding new ways to express who you are through the body you now have. As Merla discovered, keeping active through creative pursuits - whether it's painting, music, or gentle movement - helps maintain both physical and mental well-being.

Remember: These changes are not the end of the story - they're just new chapters in the ongoing narrative of your life. The body may change, but the spirit within can continue to grow, adapt, and even thrive.

Finding Grace in Letting Go

The art of letting go becomes more profound with each passing year. Like the changing seasons in our garden, we've learned that release is as natural as growth - and just as necessary for continued vitality.

Evita: After watching countless friends struggle against the inevitable changes of aging, I've discovered that those who age most gracefully are those who master the art of gentle release. Just as autumn leaves don't cling desperately to their branches, we too must learn when to hold on and when to let go.

Lionel: The most valuable lesson I've learned about letting go came from observing my great friend Bob who showed us how to face life's changes with humor and adaptability ̈ When circumstances required him to move into a care home – a time of life we all dread if we fear institutionalisation and dependence - he chose to see it as 'living in a 5-star hotel' rather than lamenting his losses.

Letting go isn't about giving up - it's about making space for what remains truly important.

We've found that releasing our grip on certain aspects of life allows us to hold more tightly to what matters most:

- **Release perfectionism to embrace authenticity.**

- **Let go of rigid expectations to welcome surprise.**

- **Surrender the need to control everything to find peace in acceptance.**

- **Release old grudges to make room for joy.**

- **Let go of outdated self-images to discover who you are now.**

The process requires both courage and humility. It means acknowledging that we can't hold onto everything - our youth, our independence, our loved ones - forever. But in that acknowledgment lies a profound freedom.

Evita: I remember struggling to accept help with tasks I'd always managed alone. My pride resisted, but wisdom whispered that accepting assistance wasn't weakness - it was adaptation. Now I see that letting others help actually strengthens our connections and creates opportunities for meaningful exchange.

Lionel: And I've learned that letting go of my need to be constantly productive has allowed me to discover the joy of simply being present. Like our fellow nonagenarians who credit their longevity to simple pleasures and laughter rather than rigid regimens, we've found that releasing expectations often leads to unexpected gifts.

Perhaps the most important aspect of letting go is maintaining your sense of humor through the process. As we've observed in long-lived individuals, those who can laugh at life's changes tend to weather them better than those who resist every transition.

The grace in letting go comes not from the release itself, but from how we choose to view it. Each release can be seen as a loss or as an opening - a chance to discover new ways of being, new forms of joy, new definitions of purpose.

Remember, letting go isn't about losing yourself - it's about discovering which parts are truly essential and which you can release with grace. Like the seasons themselves, change is inevitable. The art lies in learning to flow with it rather than against it.

Living Fully While Accepting Mortality

The greatest wisdom about mortality often comes from those who've lived long enough to see it clearly. At ninety-five, we've learned that accepting death's inevitability doesn't diminish life - it enhances it.

Evita: Someone had the audacity to ask me recently if I was afraid of dying. I told them I'm too busy living to worry about that just yet. That's the secret - not denial of death, but full engagement with life. What I've come to believe is that death isn't the opposite of life - it's part of it. The real question isn't how long we live, but how well we inhabit the time we have.

(And by the way, I am not afraid of dying!)

When I was 18 years old, I had a dream that I'd died, and it was the most peaceful and relaxing feeling ever, like dropping off into the deepest, most beautiful sleep. Since that dream, I've never feared death. No matter what happens during our final moments, that feeling of slipping away was, well, I'd say, absolute bliss.

Lionel: Yes, I remember you telling me about that dream all those eons ago, so I don't fear the inevitable either. Accepting mortality doesn't mean becoming solemn. Humor can coexist with the awareness of life's finite nature. Embracing each day with positivity while acknowledging mortality creates a special kind of freedom.

We've discovered that living fully while accepting mortality involves several key principles.

- **Embrace each day as a gift, not a guarantee.**

- **Maintain humor and lightness about aging.**

- **Stay engaged with life through meaningful activities.**

- **Share wisdom and stories with younger generations.**

- **Focus on quality of life rather than quantity.**

Like Raymonde and Lucienne, the record-holding oldest twins, we've found that regular enjoyment of simple pleasures - playing cards, dancing, maintaining friendships - keeps life vibrant even as we acknowledge its temporal nature.

Evita: The paradox we've discovered is that accepting mortality actually makes life richer. When you stop pretending that you'll live forever, you start appreciating the miracle of each ordinary day. The morning coffee tastes better. The sunset looks more beautiful. Even mundane moments carry a subtle glow of preciousness.

Lionel: We probably sound like broken old records, but it's about choosing to live fully within the time we have. Being open about mortality doesn't diminish our capacity for life - it deepens it.

Our ability to maintain that zest while acknowledging our advanced age exemplifies true wisdom about living fully while accepting mortality.

We've observed that those who age most gracefully aren't those who fight against mortality, but those who accept it while remaining engaged with life. Like our fellow nonagenarian twins who maintained their social connections and sense of humor well into their nineties, we've found that acceptance creates space for joy rather than diminishing it.

The key is balance - acknowledging mortality without being consumed by it. We plan for tomorrow while savoring today. We make peace with our limitations while celebrating our continuing capabilities. We acknowledge loss while remaining open to new experiences and connections.

Remember: Every morning is a gift, every sunset a blessing, and every moment in between an opportunity to live fully, love deeply, and laugh heartily - not in spite of mortality, but because of it. This awareness doesn't cast a shadow over life; it illuminates its precious nature.

The Quiet Power of Acceptance

As we close this chapter on resilience and mortality, we're reminded that true strength often lies not in resistance, but in acceptance. Through our nine-plus decades of living, we've discovered that making peace with change and mortality isn't about giving up - it's about opening up to life's natural rhythms.

Evita: The most profound lesson I've learned about acceptance came when I stopped fighting against my aging reflection and started seeing it as a map of a life well-lived. Each line tells a story of laughter, worry, or wonder. Now when I look in the mirror, I don't see loss - I see history.

Lionel: And I've found that accepting my limitations has actually expanded my world rather than shrinking it. When I could no longer bend to tend my beloved roses, I put in vertical climbing ones! Life always offers alternatives if we're willing to adapt.

We've learned that resilience isn't about maintaining everything exactly as it was - it's about finding new ways to flourish within each phase of life. Like our garden, which changes with each season yet remains vibrant in its own way, we too must learn to bloom differently as time passes.

The art of acceptance involves several key understandings:

- **Change is not your enemy - it's life's natural rhythm.**

- **Adaptation is not surrender - it's wisdom in action.**

- **Making peace with mortality enhances life rather than diminishing it.**

- **Gratitude grows stronger when we stop taking time for granted.**

- **Joy becomes deeper when we accept its transient nature.**

Through our years of watching friends and family navigate their own journeys with aging, we've observed that those who resist change often suffer more than those who learn to flow with it. The body may protest, but the spirit can grow more supple with each passing season.

Evita: In accepting my mortality, I've found an unexpected freedom. I no longer waste energy pretending I'll live forever. Instead, I pour that energy into living fully now - into savoring my morning coffee, into really listening when friends speak, into noticing the smell of rain after a drought.

Lionel: Yes, and in making peace with change, we've discovered that each phase of life offers its own unique gifts. We may not run marathons anymore, but we've developed a deeper appreciation for life's quiet moments and simple pleasures.

As we close this reflection on resilience and acceptance, remember that making peace with change and mortality isn't about surrendering to them - it's about embracing the full spectrum of life's experiences. It's about understanding that every season has its purpose, every change its wisdom to impart.

The greatest paradox we've discovered is that accepting our mortality doesn't diminish life - it enhances it. When we stop pretending that we'll live forever, we start truly living now. And that, perhaps, is the deepest wisdom age has to offer.

What We Know Now

- **If you're young, don't waste time trying to be perfect.**

- **Be curious. Be kind. Move. Eat. Laugh. And every now and then, make a small fool of yourself on purpose — it's a fine stretch for the soul.**

- **If you're old, remember you're still becoming someone. You may just be doing it a little more quietly.**

- **Stay interested in living, even as you prepare to leave; that's the difference between growing old and simply getting older.**

- **And when the day comes that we don't wake up — well, we hope it's after breakfast. We've come this far; we might as well go on a full stomach.**

Our Rule for Longevity #12:

Carry less as you go. The lighter your heart, the longer your journey. Because in the end, it's not about how long we live, but how fully we inhabit each moment we're given.

CHAPTER 13

The SuperAger Within

YOU COULD BE ONE

Memory is the echo of a life still paying attention.

– John W. Campbell Jr.

Every so often, science finally catches up with what some old souls have known all along: age may wrinkle the skin, but it doesn't have to wrinkle the mind.

Researchers at Northwestern University in Chicago identified a remarkable group of people they call SuperAgers — men and women in their eighties whose memory and attention rival those of people in their fifties. These individuals don't just 'age well.' They redefine age.

The Science of Staying Sharp

When neuroscientists examined the brains of SuperAgers, they found something astonishing: their brains looked biologically younger. The outer layer — the cortex — had not thinned with time as it typically does. In fact, some regions, particularly the anterior cingulate cortex (responsible for decision-making and motivation), were thicker than in many middle-aged adults.

The real surprise, though, lay in the microscopic details. Their brains contained fewer of the toxic amyloid and tau proteins — the ones that tangle up neurons and lead to Alzheimer's.

Even more remarkable, some SuperAgers had those proteins but seemed unbothered by them. Their minds carried on, unfazed. Scientists now speak of two kinds of protection: resistance (they don't form the tangles) and resilience (they do, but don't suffer for it).

Their brains also contained more Von Economo neurons — rare cells thought to help with intuition, empathy, and quick social judgment.

These may explain why SuperAgers are often described as lively conversationalists, curious listeners, and people with an instinct for connection.

The Human Element

That, it seems, is the real common thread. Despite differing diets, exercise habits, or genetic luck, SuperAgers tend to live socially rich lives. They have strong interpersonal relationships. They're joiners, connectors, chatters, storytellers. They belong — to families, clubs, choirs, church groups, bridge tables.

It fits beautifully with what we've already explored in earlier chapters: that movement, humour, and emotional flexibility all feed longevity, but connection gives it meaning. The emotional immune system we spoke of — that ability to laugh and let go — may in fact be part of this same protective architecture. A calm, curious, socially engaged mind seems to build literal neural resilience.

Case Study

Our friend Lizzie, like us, has never seen herself as exceptional. She raised three children, taught school, read voraciously, and kept a small circle of friends who met every Friday for coffee and cryptic crosswords.

A widow at 90, she still drives (only by daylight), but her recall is astounding. She remembers the birthdays of all ten grandchildren and the names of their pets.

When she took part in a local memory study, researchers were startled — Lizzie performed like someone thirty years younger. Yet her daily life offers few mysteries. She walks to the shops, cooks her own meals, reads history books "to see where we've gone wrong," and calls at least one friend every day "just to check they're still breathing, or to let them know I am".

Her secret, she insists, isn't Sudoku or supplements. "It's people," she says. "If I ever stop caring about people, I'll probably forget who I am."

Lizzie doesn't ignore emotional boundaries. She sees them as a form of self-care, having learned to comfort others without absorbing their sorrow.

Her doctor believes her social rhythm — that daily cognitive dance of empathy, conversation, and laughter — has kept her brain supple. She's a living example of what science is only now putting names to: connection as cognitive preservation

Lessons from the SuperAgers

What SuperAgers teach us isn't to chase youth, but to keep participating in life. Keep moving, thinking, engaging, learning. Keep saying yes. Your brain, like a beloved car, runs best when used often and with joy.

As one 86-year-old SuperAger put it after another round of memory tests:

"Longevity, after all, isn't merely surviving the years. It's staying alert within them — able to learn a new name, find the right word, remember a song lyric, or recall the smell of your grandmother's kitchen without the fog of forgetting".

Another one put it: "I don't have time to forget things — I'm too busy remembering people."

That may be the truest formula of all: stay busy remembering.

Could You Be a SuperAger?

If you're wondering whether you might qualify as a SuperAger yourself, the answer doesn't come from a brain scan or a lab test. It's written in how you live – in your habits, your humor, your curiosity, and your connections.

The scientists at Northwestern may measure cortex thickness, but the rest of us can look for simpler clues – the kind you can spot in your daily life.

Five signs you might be one already:

- **You remember names — and stories.**

- **You stay curious.**

- **You move, but you don't obsess.**

- **You laugh easily — especially at yourself.**

- **You stay connected.**

A thick cortex is good, a thick skin even better.

You phone friends. You show up. You listen and you're listened to.

SuperAgers thrive in the rich soup of human contact – proof that a good conversation is as stimulating as any crossword.

SuperAgers don't just recall faces; they remember that Tom's daughter just moved to Perth and that she's allergic to mangoes. It's not photographic memory — it's relational memory. You care, therefore you recall.

Whether it's learning how to use AirTags, following world news, or asking your grandson what on earth "rizz" means, curiosity keeps the neural lights on. The brain loves novelty — it's how it knows you're still interested in living.

SuperAgers are active, not athletic. They garden, dance, stroll, stretch. They move for joy, not for data. The goal isn't 10,000 steps — it's motion with meaning.

Emotional resilience, humour, and perspective are all part of the Super-Ager toolkit.

Our Rule for Longevity #13:

The SuperAger's motto: Keep talking. Keep laughing. Keep learning. Forget to retire from life.

CHAPTER 14

Looking Forward

LIVING THE BONUS YEARS

When you're over the hill, you begin to pick up speed.

– Charles Schulz

When people ask us what it feels like to be 'up there', almost 100, we tell them we're living in bonus time. Like a public holiday when you work full-time, or a day without appointments, these bonuses of time come as a privilege. They are unexpected gifts that offer us unique opportunities to witness, to share, and to appreciate life's continuing unfolding.

This work of ours is part reflection, part quiet celebration. We are two voices of those who have truly lived and are now in a position to impart a final, simple truth: that longevity is not only about years added to life, but life added to years.

If there's one thing ninety-five years will teach you, it's this: life isn't meant to be rushed — it's meant to be savored. When you are young, you race. You chase deadlines, dreams, people, possessions. But the older you get, the more you realise that the good moments were never the spectacular ones — they were the small ones. The smell of a slow-cooked meal, the warmth of the sun peeking through on a cool day, the familiar laugh of someone you love.

That's what stays. That's what nourishes you long after the noise fades.

These days, we move more slowly, but we notice more. We taste our food properly. We listen to the different bird songs. We observe how the light changes from hour to hour. We've come to understand that slowing down isn't losing time — it's reclaiming it.

We used to think 'a full life' meant cramming in as much activity as possible. Now we know it means feeling as much as possible — fully, deeply, consciously. Each additional day is an unexpected gift, carrying both wonder and wisdom in its quiet unfolding.

In this chapter, we'll explore what it means to live fully in these bonus years, embracing each day with gratitude and purpose. We'll share our insights on maintaining independence with grace, creating lasting legacies through daily choices, and finding joy in life's continuing journey.

Because we've learned that the real measure of longevity isn't just in the counting of years, but in how richly we inhabit each moment we're given.

Embracing Each Day as a Gift

Every day is a bonus at our age, and the art of embracing each day as a gift becomes clearer with age.

Lionel: Every morning brings its own small miracles, the first one being that I woke up!

Evita: I've developed what I call my 'morning inventory' - not of what I need to do, but of what I already have. Good legs that still carry me (even if they complain a bit), eyes that can read (with help from my glasses), and another day to add to my collection. This practice isn't about positive thinking; it's about accurate thinking. 'Up here', each day truly is a gift that many of our peers haven't received.

We've discovered that embracing each day means accepting it completely - with its aches and pains, its surprises and disappointments. Some mornings are harder than others, but even difficult days carry their own gifts: lessons in patience, opportunities for rest, or moments of unexpected kindness.

The trick is to stay present. Not to wish for yesterday's strength or tomorrow's plans, but to fully inhabit today. We've outlived many who were always waiting for 'someday' - someday when they'd have more time, more money, more energy. But we've learned that 'someday' is a thief that steals today's joy.

Here's what we've learned about making each day count:

- **Start with gratitude - not just thinking it, but speaking it aloud.**

- **Find humor in small moments - laughter is a way of saying 'yes' to life.**

- **Create simple rituals that give each day its shape.**

- **Stay connected - share your day with others, even briefly.**

- **Notice beauty in ordinary things.**

Lionel: Recently, I caught myself complaining about having to water the garden yet again. Then I stopped and thought: I may be ancient, but I'm still strong enough to move a hose around. What a gift!

That's when I realized - it's not about what we *have* to do, but what we *get* to do.

We've learned that embracing each day isn't about grand gestures or ambitious plans. It's about presence, appreciation, and the quiet joy of still being here.

Every morning is an unexpected gift, and every evening is a small victory. That's not just optimism - at ninety-five, it's simply the truth.

Evita: My granddaughter teases us for bragging about our age. "It's because we've earned it!', we say. And we're truly proud to have both made it this far.

Maintaining Independence with Grace

Independence in our nineties isn't about doing everything alone - it's about knowing when to ask for help and when to stand firm in our capabilities. We maintain our vitality through a combination of mutual support and determined self-reliance. We've learned that grace comes from finding the right balance.

Evita: I remember watching my mother stubbornly refuse help until she couldn't manage at all. That taught me something valuable: independence isn't about proving yourself - it's about preserving yourself. Now I accept help with heavy lifting and home maintenance, which allows me to save my energy for the activities that bring me joy and maintain my autonomy.

Here's what we've learned about maintaining independence with grace:

- **Adapt your environment, don't fight it.** Install handrails, improve lighting, rearrange furniture for easy navigation.

- **Keep essential items within easy reach.**

- **Embrace helpful technologies while maintaining traditional skills.**

- **Establish routines that support self-sufficiency.**

- **Accept help that preserves energy for what matters most.**

The physical aspects of independence require attention and care. Mental agility plays an equally crucial role. We keep our minds sharp through continuous learning and adaptation. Whether it's mastering new technologies or pursuing creative hobbies, each new skill reinforces our ability to navigate life independently.

Lionel: I've learned that independence doesn't mean isolation. Living next door to my sister allows us to support each other while maintaining our separate spaces. This arrangement provides security without sacrificing autonomy.

Evita: It's funny. Last year, Lionel and I celebrated our first shared birthday since our 21st! We hadn't even realised it. We've always been close, but until recently, not geographically. My life took me overseas for decades. We had separate lives and families. Life got in the way, as they say. We caught up as often as we could but our paths never seemed to cross at birthday time. Now we're next-door-neighbours, and almost as inseparable as we were as children. It's funny how things turn out.

Maintaining independence requires both physical and emotional strategies:

- **Regular physical activity tailored to our abilities.**

- **Daily self-care routines that reinforce autonomy.**

- **Strong social networks that provide support when needed.**

- **Continuous learning and adaptation to new situations.**

- **A positive attitude that focuses on capabilities rather than limitations.**

Remember: independence at ninety-five isn't about doing everything yourself - it's about maintaining control over your daily life while accepting help that enhances rather than diminishes your autonomy. It's about making choices that preserve your energy for what matters most to you.

As we often say, true independence is knowing when to stand firm and when to lean on others - and having the wisdom to tell the difference.

The secret is to focus on what we can do rather than what we can't. Every morning, we make our own beds, prepare our own meals, and plan our own days. These simple acts of self-reliance build upon each other, creating a foundation of independence that supports our well-being.

Creating Legacy Through Daily Choices

The most profound legacy we can leave isn't built in grand gestures or material wealth, but in the quiet accumulation of daily choices that shape both our lives and those around us. We've discovered that our greatest impact often comes from simply living our values consistently, day after day.

Here's what we've learned about creating lasting legacy through daily choices:

- **Embrace authenticity over perfection** - like the Tipton Twins' candid sharing of their quirky preferences and honest perspectives.

- **Maintain physical vitality through consistent, age-appropriate movement.**

- **Stay open to new experiences and learning, regardless of age.**

- **Foster connections that span generations.**

- **Share wisdom with humor and humility.**

We've discovered that legacy isn't something you leave behind - it's something you live every day. Through our own experience and observing others, we've seen how seemingly small choices accumulate to create lasting impact.

Lionel: I used to think legacy was about leaving behind something impressive - achievements, wealth, or grand accomplishments. But watching the Tipton Twins share their simple daily routines and joy for life with millions of followers showed me that true legacy is built in small, consistent choices that inspire others.

Evita: In case you hadn't noticed, Lionel has a real thing for the Tipton Twins! Their teachers were amazed, but what struck me most was how their daily commitment to movement inspired thousands of others to stay active.

Lionel: Their viral fame wasn't planned; it emerged naturally from their authentic way of living and willingness to share their daily experiences. That's legacy in action - not through preaching, but through living example. We hope, by putting together this book, that we can be a fraction as inspiring.

We've learned that staying open to new experiences keeps us growing and contributing. Every time we try something new, we show others that age needn't limit curiosity or learning.

Creating legacy through daily choices involves:

- **Maintaining physical health through regular movement, even if modified for age.**

- **Staying mentally engaged and open to new learning.**

- **Fostering meaningful connections across generations.**

- **Sharing wisdom with humor and authenticity.**

- **Embracing each day as an opportunity to inspire others.**

Lionel: Recently, I overheard my grandson telling his friend, "My grandad still paints every day and posts his art online."

That's when I realized - legacy isn't about what we leave behind, it's about how we live right now. Every brush stroke, every shared meal, every kind word becomes part of the story we're writing with our lives.

Our legacy isn't written in stone - it's written in the lives we touch, the examples we set, and the joy we share, one day at a time.

Looking Back, Looking Forward

As we conclude this chapter on living in the bonus years, we're reminded of a truth that has become clearer with each passing decade: longevity isn't just about adding years to life, but adding life to years.

Through our exploration of embracing each day as a gift, maintaining independence with grace, and creating legacy through daily choices, we've shared what ninety-five years have taught us about living fully in what we call 'bonus time.'

The journey has shown us that these extra years aren't just a gift - they're an opportunity. An opportunity to witness, to share, to appreciate, and most importantly, to continue growing. Like the garden we still tend, life keeps offering new seasons of bloom, even in what others might consider winter.

We've learned that:

- **Every morning is a blank canvas, waiting to be painted with purpose and gratitude.**

- **Independence comes from knowing when to stand firm and when to accept help.**

- **Legacy isn't built in grand gestures, but in daily choices that reflect our values.**

- **Joy multiplies when shared, and purpose deepens with each passing year.**

- **The best way to honor these bonus years is to live them fully, mindfully, and gratefully**

Perhaps the most profound lesson we've gained in our ninety-five years is this: life doesn't diminish with age - it distills. Like fine wine, it becomes richer, more complex, more precious with each passing year.

We don't know how many more mornings we'll have the privilege to welcome, but we know this - we'll greet each one with the same mixture of gratitude and curiosity that has carried us this far. Because we've learned that every day truly is a bonus, and how we choose to live it matters more than how many we're given.

As we close this chapter, we invite you to join us in viewing each day not as a given, but as a gift. Because the real secret to longevity isn't in how long you live, but in how fully you embrace each moment you're given.

Still here.

Still grateful.

Still amazed.

Our Rule for Longevity #14:

Capture the essence of living well in these bonus years. Savour everything - the taste, the silence, the laughter, the rain. A well-lived life is simply one that has been noticed.

CHAPTER 15

Habits That Help Longevity

A PRACTICAL LIST

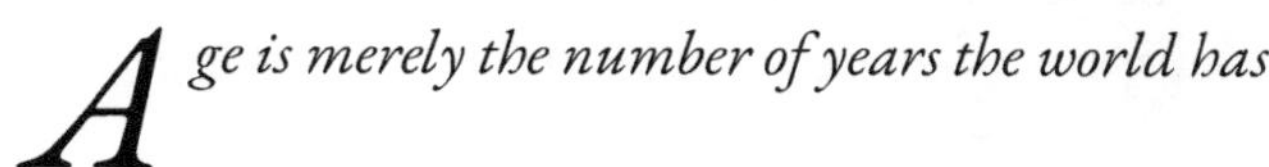

Age is merely the number of years the world has been enjoying you.

– Unknown

Longevity isn't a mystery — it's a series of small, mostly sensible choices, repeated until they turn into character.

Here are thirty that have served us well. We can't promise immortality, but we can promise improvement.

1. Move a little — every day.

The day you stop moving is the day the furniture starts winning.

2. Get sunlight before noon.

If you wake up late, open the curtains and pretend.

3. Stretch something — body or patience.

Both tighten if neglected.

4. Keep meals simple, colourful, and shared.

A dinner table is better medicine than most pills.

5. Drink water before wine.

It doesn't ruin the wine, and it does improve the morning after.

6. Sleep like it's your job.

Because it is. That's when your body files away all your nonsense.

7. Nap if needed, but don't move in.

Short naps refresh; long ones make you forget what century it is.

8. Take stairs when you can.

They're free and unadvertised fitness equipment.

9. Learn something new every year.

It keeps the neurons limber and the ego humble.

10. Laugh daily — bonus points if it's at yourself.

Vanity ages faster than skin.

11. Eat a vegetable that still looks like a vegetable.

If it glows or crunches in unnatural ways, reconsider. (Potato chips and ketchup don't count).

12. Sit with silence.

Noise can fill a room. Only silence fills a person.

13. Keep one small promise to yourself every day.

It builds self-respect better than any guru's advice.

14. Say "no" without explaining.

Polite, firm, final. You'll gain hours of peace.

15. Find your tribe, even if it's just one other misfit.

Human beings last longer in pairs and groups, like batteries.

16. Tend to something that can't talk back.

A plant, a pet, a sourdough starter — all teach patience and humility.

17. Spend time with people younger than you.

Borrow their curiosity. Ignore their slang.

18. Spend time with people older than you.

They'll remind you what truly matters — and what doesn't.

19. Forgive quickly but remember kindly.

Forgetfulness is a gift; grace is a habit.

20. Keep your sense of humour sharper than your eyesight.

One will fail before the other.

21. Don't believe everything you think.

Brains are noisy places; not all thoughts deserve your attention.

22. Treat worry like a short-term guest

Let it visit, not move in.

23. Write things down.

Lists, memories, names — it's how the mind tidies itself.

24. Complain less than you compliment.

People will start inviting you places again.

25. Learn when to leave a party.

Or a job. Or an argument. Staying too long spoils everything.

26. Keep your curiosity greater than your criticism.

That alone will keep you interesting — and alive.

27. Don't measure life in years.

Measure it in stories. That's the real currency of age.

28. Smile at strangers — especially the grumpy ones.

It confuses them, which is reward enough.

29. Be stubborn about gratitude.

Find one thing every day that didn't go wrong.

30. Say thank you — for everything, even this moment.

Because one day, you'll wish for another just like it.

Rule for Longevity #15:

Always remind yourself that longevity isn't about adding years to your life — it's about keeping your life alive in the years you have.

There's no trick to it, really. Just curiosity, movement, humour, and a daily refusal to give up being delighted.

Chapter 16

Reflections

from the Far End of the Long Road

The longer I live, the more beautiful life becomes.

– Frank Lloyd Wright

Being in our nineties is like living on a mountain — the air is thinner, the view is better, and you move a little slower because you don't want to fall off.

After over nine decades of living, learning, and loving, we've discovered that the true secret to longevity isn't found in expensive supplements, complicated exercise routines, or the latest wellness trends. It's woven into the simple, daily choices we make and the attitudes we cultivate.

Through these chapters, we've shared our journey - not as experts with degrees, but as living testimonies to what actually works. We've explored the importance of movement without obsession, nourishment without complexity, and rest without guilt. We've discussed how maintaining purpose, nurturing connections, and keeping our minds engaged have contributed to our longevity.

The emotional immune system we've developed - through laughter, forgiveness, and letting go - has proven as vital as any physical exercise. We've learned that resilience isn't about avoiding change but embracing it with grace. And perhaps most importantly, we've discovered that these bonus years are not a burden but a gift to be savored.

As we reflect on our journey, we're struck by how simple the formula for longevity really is. The great secret of longevity isn't hidden in a laboratory or a lecture. It's tucked into the ordinary moments that everyone overlooks. You don't notice you're collecting these moments until they become your real wealth.

What We'd Tell Our Younger Selves

If we could send a message back to our twenty-year-old selves, we'd need to start with an apology.

"Sorry," we'd say, "you were right about a few things — but only a few."

The rest, you learn the long way: through wrong turns, lost keys, bad haircuts, and the kind of love that teaches rather than lasts.

Longevity isn't just surviving the years; it's learning what's worth surviving for.

So, to our younger selves — and perhaps to you — here's what we've learned in nine long, beautiful, ridiculous decades:

1. Don't Chase Perfection — It Ages Faster Than You Do

Perfection is a moving target, usually held by someone else.

Do things well enough and then get on with living. No one remembers the crooked table you built — they remember the meal you served on it.

Perfect is the enemy of good.

2. Move Every Day, Even If It's Just Away from Negativity

Exercise is fine. Dancing in the kitchen is better. The body likes movement, but the soul likes rhythm — so give it both.

3. Don't Confuse Busy with Useful

In your thirties, you'll think exhaustion is a badge of honour. It isn't.

Rest isn't laziness; it's refuelling. The religious souls among us know that even God took a day off.

4. Learn to Listen Without Waiting for Your Turn to Talk

It's the cheapest wisdom there is.

People reveal their entire philosophy between two sentences — if you stop rehearsing yours long enough to hear it.

5. Fear Makes Terrible Decisions

Fear will tell you to play safe, stay quiet, avoid heartbreak. Ignore it.

The worst pain isn't failure — it's wondering what might've happened if you'd said yes.

6. Laugh Loudly, Especially at Yourself

Pride is heavy. Laughter travels light.

When you can giggle at your own foolishness, you're halfway to grace — and easier company.

7. Collect People, Not Possessions

The furniture won't visit you in hospital. But the friend you made by sharing an umbrella might.

8. Apologise Quickly, Even If You're Only 30% at Fault

It's astonishing how much peace you can buy with a single honest "sorry." Keep a few ready — you'll need them.

9. Don't Wait for Joy to Knock

Invite it in, often.

Sometimes it looks like a walk, a dog, or a slice of cake. Other times it looks like you, remembering to notice.

10. Growing Old Is Not a Decline — It's a Reveal

Age doesn't strip us down; it peels us back to who we really are. You stop pretending, stop apologising, stop performing.

And one morning, you realise you've become entirely yourself — the person you were meant to be before you got distracted by everything else.

What We Know for Certain

Life isn't about how long it lasts — it's about how much of it you notice.

And longevity isn't the goal. It's the side effect of living with purpose, humour, and a little bit of stubborn hope.

So, eat your porridge, walk your miles, forgive what you can, and laugh when you shouldn't.

If you're lucky, you'll grow old enough to discover what a miracle that is.

And when you do, write it down. Someone younger than you needs to hear it.

Reflection

These aren't revolutionary insights, but they are time-tested truths. They've carried us through close to a century of changes, challenges, and celebrations.

But perhaps our most valuable lesson has been this: It's about staying engaged with the world even as it changes around you.

To those who aspire to longevity, we say this: don't chase years - chase experiences. Don't count time - make time count. And remember that the best anti-aging secret isn't found in a bottle or a gym - it's found in the way you choose to live each day.

We hope this book has shown that living well into your nineties isn't about defying age - it's about embracing it with grace, humor, and purpose. It's about understanding that every day is a gift, not a guarantee.

Our Rule for Longevity #16:

Always try to maintain the curiosity of a child while accumulating the wisdom of age.

CHAPTER 17

The Art of Leaving Well

THE CHAPTER NO ONE WANTS TO WRITE

Do not act as if you are going to live ten thousand years. Death hangs over you. While you live, while it is in your power, be good.

- Marcus Aurelius

We talk a lot about how to live longer, but very little about how to stop living — gracefully, consciously, and without fear.

Evita: No-one likes to think about dying. We talk about 'passing,' 'crossing over,' or 'slipping away' — as if death were a minor social embarrassment, best handled quietly and out of sight. It's as if silence can keep death waiting politely at the door. Yet death, like an old acquaintance, will always find a way to knock.

Lionel: But here's the truth: if you've made it this far in the book, you've already earned the right to talk about it.

After all, longevity isn't about outsmarting death — it's about making peace with it.

Living well and leaving well are part of the same conversation. One is the practice; the other is the performance.

Preparing for the end of life isn't morbid; it's an act of love — for yourself and those who remain. The people who die most peacefully aren't those who fought hardest against mortality, but those who learned to make peace with it. They leave behind order instead of chaos, tenderness instead of turmoil.

A good death doesn't happen by accident. It's the natural continuation of a good life: one lived with awareness, gratitude, and care for others.

We tidy up our homes before guests arrive; it makes sense to do the same before we go. That doesn't mean giving up — it means setting things right, so that love and memory can take the place of fear.

A good death isn't an accident. It's the natural continuation of a good life — one lived with awareness, humility, and dignity.

A Note on Mortality

The older we get, the more the topic shifts from abstract to personal. Friends start disappearing from Christmas lists. We catch ourselves saying, "At our age…" with the quiet understanding that time has become precious currency.

Yet there's nothing grim about acknowledging mortality. It's clarifying. It makes the colours of life sharper, the laughter louder, the gratitude deeper. Death, in its odd way, is the great editor — it reminds us what to keep and what to let go.

So this section is not about endings. It's about completion.

It's about leaving behind less mess and more meaning.

It's about dignity, empathy, and the art of a graceful exit.

If you've spent your whole life learning how to live, this is simply the final lesson — how to leave with the same generosity and good humour that carried you this far.

Facing the Final Chapter: Accepting Mortality Without Fear

We spend most of our lives trying to ignore death. In childhood, it's a distant shadow — abstract, almost unreal. In middle age, it's a cautionary tale whispered in health articles and statistics. By the time we reach our later years, it's no longer hypothetical. Friends leave. Parents fade. The mirror reminds us that our bodies are wearing out.

Yet the truth is simple: you cannot escape it. And pretending you can is exhausting. The people who age well — and die well — have discovered that acceptance is not surrender. It's preparation. They have their paperwork in order, their words of love spoken, their grudges trimmed down to size.

They go not because they've given up, but because they've given enough. It's living with your eyes open, even when what you see is uncomfortable.

Why Acceptance Matters

Acceptance of mortality doesn't mean giving up on life. Far from it. It's about understanding that life has limits and learning to work within them. People who accept death's inevitability often find they can live more fully in the present. They laugh louder, forgive faster, and notice the small delights that slip by the fearful or the distracted.

Acceptance allows us to prioritize what matters. It's easier to let go of petty grievances, to choose joy over perfection, to spend time with the people and projects that bring us true satisfaction. And when the end comes, they are ready. Not eager, perhaps, but calm — and that calm is contagious, comforting, and profoundly wise.

Facing Fear with Honesty

Evita: I know I said earlier that I wasn't afraid of dying. I think my fear is more about running out of time.

Fear of death is universal, and it wears many disguises: anxiety, denial, obsession with health, or even relentless busyness. The older we get, the more we realize that these are simply attempts to hold on to something we cannot.

One of the best ways to meet this fear is to name it. Speak about it. Write about it. Sit with it. Fear, when acknowledged, loses much of its power. It shrinks in the light of attention, replaced by clarity and compassion.

Those who make peace with fear do not pretend it doesn't exist. They simply learn to walk alongside it, like an uncomfortable but necessary companion, without letting it dictate their every choice.

Practical ways to prepare emotionally:

- **Talk openly** — With family, friends, or a trusted confidante. Sharing your thoughts about death is not morbid; it's honest.

- **Write your reflections** — Journaling or letters can externalize fears and regrets, leaving you freer to focus on gratitude.

- **Reflect on your legacy** — Consider what matters most to you, and how you can leave small tokens, words, or stories that outlast your presence.

- **Practise small acts of closure** — Reconciling with estranged friends, apologizing where needed, forgiving grievances — even tiny ones — can bring profound emotional relief.

- **Develop rituals of mindfulness** — Meditation, quiet walks, or simple breathing exercises help cultivate peace of mind, so that when the inevitable comes, you meet it with awareness, not panic.

The Upside of Knowing the End is Near

Facing mortality can feel heavy at first, but paradoxically, it lightens life. People who know their time is finite often live with more intention, love more openly, and savor experiences more deeply.

There's a certain freedom in knowing there is a horizon. You can choose to waste less time on meaningless conflicts. You can choose to embrace joy more fully, to laugh harder, to notice beauty even in ordinary moments.

Ultimately, accepting mortality transforms life from a battle against time into a conversation with it. And those who master that conversation experience a serenity that eludes most — a quiet readiness that will carry them through their final chapter with grace.

No one wants to die, yet everyone wants to live. Acceptance allows us to have both: the courage to embrace the days we have left, and the peace to let go when the time comes. It's the first and most important step in learning how to leave well — a lesson in humility, perspective, and the quiet art of living fully until the very end.

The Courage to Talk About It

Few families talk openly about death until it's too late. We avoid it out of love — we don't want to upset each other. Yet this silence can be the cruelest thing of all.

Evita: There's a strange relief in naming the unnameable. Once someone says, "Let's talk about what happens when I'm not here," the tension in the room changes. The subject stops being a shadow and becomes something manageable, even practical.

Having the conversation is not about dying sooner; it's about living honestly. It is not to hasten death — it's to humanise it, clearing the air of fear and confusion, and turning dread into dialogue.

Say what you want — where you'd like to be, what comforts you, what frightens you, what makes you feel human. These aren't medical decisions so much as personal ones. Talk about your wishes: comfort, music, visitors, even humour. Talk about what matters most in your last days. Clarity is the ultimate kindness.

Lionel: You may find your family resists, but later they'll be grateful. Nothing brings peace like clarity. In the end, the conversation you avoided may be the one that gives everyone strength.

The Gift of Dignity: Choosing How to Leave

Dignity is one of those words we use easily, but it becomes harder to define as life wanes. It's not about appearances, or control over others, or even independence in the usual sense. At the end of life, dignity is something far more personal: it's the quiet affirmation that you are still yourself, even as the world and your body remind you of your limits.

To leave well is to leave with dignity. It's not about prolonging life at all costs, nor is it about dramatics or heroics. It's about making choices that reflect who you are, what you value, and how you want to be remembered — without fear, shame, or coercion.

Dignity means being heard, seen, and respected. It's the freedom to decide what comfort looks like, what care means, and when enough is enough.It's about agency, empathy, and the courage to say, "This is who I am, and this is how I wish to go."

A dignified death, like a dignified life, comes from authenticity — living and leaving in accordance with your own values.

To go with dignity is to remain yourself until the last moment — to be seen as a whole person, not a patient or a burden. Dignity isn't found in machines or medication; it's in being treated as if your life still matters, even as it's ending.

Some people find peace in nature, some in faith, some in quiet acceptance. Others take comfort in knowing they still have a say — that they can choose what "enough" looks like for them.

Preparing to die well means not being ruled by fear or denial. It's about agency, kindness, and respect — both for oneself and for those left behind.

The ultimate measure of dignity isn't how long we last, but how much love we can still give and receive before the curtain falls.

What Dignity Looks Like

Dignity often appears in small acts:

- **Choosing the people who will be with you in your final days.**

- **Deciding what kind of care you want — or don't want.**

- **Expressing your wishes for comfort, for music, for privacy.**

Dignity can also show up in forgiveness — letting go of old grievances so that your final interactions are marked by love rather than resentment. And sometimes, dignity is simply the courage to speak your truth, even when it makes others uncomfortable.

The Power of Choice

The ultimate mark of dignity is autonomy. Making conscious choices — about care, about who is present, about when to accept help — restores agency when other parts of life feel out of control.

This doesn't mean you need to micromanage every detail. Small decisions, even seemingly trivial ones, can carry enormous meaning. Choosing a favorite blanket, a preferred chair, or the order in which you see loved ones — these acts signal that you are still directing your story, even as the end draws near.

Freedom of choice at life's end is not a luxury. It is a recognition of humanity, a refusal to be reduced to illness or circumstance. And it is often the last true comfort we can give ourselves.

Practical Ways to Maintain Dignity

- **Speak up about your needs and preferences** — Comfort, visitors, rituals, or music. Your voice matters until the very end.

- **Accept help without shame** — Dignity is not about going it alone; it's about being honest about what you need.

- **Set boundaries gently** — You can decide who is present and how much information is shared. It's not rude; it's self-respect.

- **Keep routines that matter** — Even small habits, like reading a favorite book or walking in the garden, reinforce continuity and identity.

- **Leave guidance for others** — Notes, letters, or recordings can provide comfort, reduce confusion, and preserve your dignity in memory.

The Emotional Benefit of Planning

Taking these steps is not only about practicality; it's about emotional well-being. People who clarify their wishes experience less fear and anxiety. Family members also benefit, because they are free from guessing or guilt. Everyone can focus on presence, not panic.

Dignity is contagious. When one person approaches the end with poise, others mirror it. The final days are marked by calmness, not chaos; clarity, not confusion; and love, not regret.

Dying with dignity isn't about perfection; it's about coherence. It's about ensuring that your final chapter reflects the life you've lived. Choosing your own path, speaking your truth, and leaving clear guidance are all acts of courage — and acts of generosity.

Ultimately, the gift of dignity is both yours and theirs: a way to finish the story on your terms, and a way to leave those you love with peace in their hearts.

The Kindness of Preparation: Putting Life in Order

Preparation is a quiet act of generosity. When we organize our affairs, both practical and emotional, we are offering a gift — not just to ourselves, but to the people who will remain. It's the difference between leaving chaos behind and leaving clarity, between adding burden and lightening hearts.

Yet preparing for the end is often avoided. Paperwork feels tedious, conversations feel awkward, and the thought of our own mortality can be uncomfortable. But the truth is that small acts of preparation can bring profound peace — to you and to those you love.

Why Preparation Matters

Preparation is not about obsessing over death. It is about ordering life. Sorting documents, clarifying wishes, leaving instructions — these are practical steps that prevent confusion and conflict. They allow family and friends to focus on presence and memory rather than decisions and logistics.

There's also a psychological benefit: preparation offers a sense of control and agency in a moment when so much feels uncertain. It transforms helplessness into action, fear into clarity, and anxiety into calm.

Areas to Consider:

- **Legal and financial matters** — Ensure wills, powers of attorney, and medical directives are up to date. Make sure key documents are easily accessible.

- **Practical arrangements** — Housing, funeral preferences, digital accounts, and personal items. Clear instructions reduce stress and second-guessing.

- **Emotional preparation** — Letters, notes, or recordings can convey thoughts and love that might otherwise go unspoken.

- **Relationships** — Small reconciliations or expressions of gratitude can leave lasting comfort for everyone.

- **Personal rituals** — Identifying music, readings, or symbolic gestures that matter to you adds meaning to the final chapter.

Leaving Lightly — The Gift of Preparation

Preparation is an act of love. It's a way of saying, "I care enough to leave things in order." It lightens the emotional load on those left behind and allows your final days to focus on connection, reflection, and comfort rather than stress or confusion.

It's also deeply empowering. Organizing life's final practicalities reminds you that you retain agency, even as your strength may fade. Every note written, every decision clarified, every conversation held is a quiet statement: I am still myself, and I can leave this world with intention.

There's a special kindness in leaving things in order. Not the grim kind of order — but the thoughtful kind that spares others confusion or regret. Putting things in order spares others the weight of uncertainty.

Write letters. Label photographs. Pass on heirlooms while you can still enjoy the giving. Give away what you no longer need. Share your passwords and your stories. Say thank you. Say sorry. Say everything that shouldn't be left unsaid.

The greatest legacy isn't money or property; it's the calm that comes from knowing you've left no emotional clutter behind.

Practical Tips for Making Preparation Kind and Manageable:

Take it one step at a time — Preparation doesn't need to be done all at once. Small, steady actions accumulate.

Engage trusted helpers — Family members, friends, or professionals can assist without taking over.

Our Rule for Longevity #17:

Think of the art of leaving well as a final act of grace.

Those who prepare to go lightly often leave a sense of serenity behind them, rather than a void.

Chapter 18

The Weight of Compassion

SUPPORTING SOMEONE WHO IS READY TO GO

Death is our friend, precisely because it brings us into absolute and passionate presence with all that is here, that is natural, that is love.

Rainer Maria Rilke, *Letters to a Young Poet*

Watching someone you love approach the end of life is one of the most delicate, emotionally challenging experiences a human being can face. You want to comfort, to protect, to persuade them to stay. Yet sometimes, the greatest kindness is simply to stand beside them without steering, guiding, or judging.

Supporting someone who is ready to let go requires courage, patience, and a gentle surrender of your own fears. It asks you to hold love in tension with acceptance, to be present without controlling, and to listen more than you speak.

Deepening the Dignity

Supporting someone who is ready to die is not about prolonging their days, but about deepening the dignity within them. When we sit with the dying without trying to fix, cheer, or contradict their readiness, we practise a form of emotional longevity: we learn that love is not measured in how long we keep someone here, but in how gently we let them go.

To support a person who is ready to die:

- **Listen more than you reassure.** Silence is sometimes the highest form of respect.

- **Ask what they need, not what you fear.**

- **Replace "Don't say that" with "I'm here."**

- **Let the conversation be honest**—death loses its sting when it's allowed to be spoken aloud.

Remember: accompaniment is an act of courage, not defeat.

In the end, the real longevity isn't only in the body that keeps breathing, but in the love that remains unbroken—even when breath is gone.

The Paradox of Compassion

Love often tempts us to intervene. We worry that if we don't push or pull, our loved one might make a mistake, suffer unnecessarily, or be lonely in their final days. But end-of-life choices are deeply personal, and trying to influence them — even with the best intentions — can unintentionally diminish their autonomy and dignity.

Compassion here is a paradox: sometimes, the kindest act is restraint. It's listening without interruption, offering comfort without imposing solutions, and simply being available — a calm anchor amid the storm of emotions.

Supporting Without Steering

It's hard to watch someone you love begin to fade. Harder still to respect their wishes when those wishes mean letting go.

When a loved one decides they're ready to stop fighting, our instinct is to argue, to plead for more time. But often what they need most is our quiet presence, not persuasion.

The greatest act of love isn't to rescue someone from their fate, but to accompany them without judgment. You can still laugh, reminisce, sing, share stories. Dying doesn't end a relationship; it simply changes its direction.

There's a subtle art to supporting someone at the end. You listen more than you speak. You affirm without advising. You create calm where fear might otherwise grow.

To be with someone in their last chapter — fully, gently — is one of life's purest privileges.

Supporting someone who is ready to go is not easy. It challenges our instincts, our fears, and our desire to protect. Yet those who learn the delicate art of accompaniment — loving without controlling — discover a profound truth: compassion is strongest when it is restrained, presence is a gift, and dignity is preserved when we honour another's choices.

Sometimes, the heaviest weight we carry is the one we do not try to lift. And sometimes, that weight, carried with love, becomes the most meaningful gift of all.

Practical ways to support without steering:

- **Affirm their agency** — Phrases like, "I'm here with you, whatever you decide" show support without pressure.

- **Stay neutral on outcomes** — Avoid comments that could be interpreted as judgment, encouragement, or disapproval.

- **Offer practical help** — Daily needs, comfort measures, or simple companionship go a long way. These are acts of love that don't compromise their choices.

- **Protect your own emotional health** — Seek support from friends, counselors, or peer groups. Being present requires stamina; you cannot pour from an empty cup.

The Emotional Risks

Supporting a loved one at this stage carries emotional weight. You may feel guilt, fear, relief, or grief — sometimes all at once. It's normal to experience complex emotions, and acknowledging them is crucial.

In some circumstances, family members may also fear suspicion or blame. It's common to worry that others might misinterpret your support as coercion or self-interest. Awareness and honesty are your best allies: keeping clear boundaries, documenting wishes if appropriate, and staying mindful of your intentions can reduce misunderstandings.

Finding Comfort Together

Even in the face of impending loss, there are moments of connection, laughter, and tenderness. Reading together, reminiscing, sharing music, or simply holding hands can create a sacred space of calm.

Presence — the quiet, unwavering presence of someone who loves — is often the greatest comfort a person can receive at the end. It allows them to face their journey with dignity and allows you to witness it without regret.

Our Longevity Rule #18:

Extend life by honoring endings – your own and those of whom you support.

CHAPTER 19

Ageing's Final Lesson

LETTING GO GRACEFULLY

I am not afraid of storms, for I am learning how to sail my ship.

- Louisa May Alcott

For most of our lives, we are taught to hold on, to accumulate, to achieve, to cling to youth, possessions, or control. Ageing, however, offers the quiet counter-lesson: the wisdom of letting go.

The emotionally resilient know that release can be as beautiful as resistance.

Letting go doesn't mean indifference. It means trusting that what mattered will endure in memory and influence.

It's laughter through tears, gratitude over grief, faith over finality.

In the same way our immune system protects our body, our emotional immune system protects our spirit. When strengthened through forgiveness, humour, and acceptance, it keeps fear at bay — even in the face of the inevitable.

A gentle death, like a gentle life, is less about control and more about surrender. Not giving up, but giving over — to love, peace, and stillness.

Letting go is not failure; it's faith. It's trust in the continuity of love, in the memory that outlasts breath.

When humour and forgiveness remain intact, even as the body weakens, something profound happens: peace arrives.

A gentle death, like a gentle life, depends less on control than on compassion — for oneself and for others.

The Freedom in Release

The older we get, the more we understand that life's weight is often in the things we try to control: opinions, grudges, appearances, outcomes. Letting go is freedom from that weight.

It doesn't diminish us; it enriches us. When we release anger, resentment, or fear, we create space for clarity, peace, and connection. Letting go is a deliberate act of self-respect and compassion — for ourselves and for others.

Practical Ways to Let Go:

- **Forgive freely** — Even minor grievances can haunt us. Letting go of them lightens the emotional load.

- **Declutter life and mind** — Simplify possessions, commitments, and mental clutter. The fewer distractions, the more focus on presence.

- **Accept help gracefully** — Needing assistance does not diminish your dignity; refusing it often diminishes your peace.

- **Release expectations** — The world does not always bend to your wishes, and neither does ageing. Accepting reality reduces suffering.

- **Prioritize meaningful connection** — Let go of trivial disputes, time-wasting obligations, and unnecessary social pressures. Invest instead in relationships and experiences that matter.

The Emotional Grace of Letting Go

Letting go is also about emotional honesty. Admit your fears, express your regrets, and articulate your desires. Speak to those you love; leave nothing unspoken that could weigh on your heart or theirs.

Humour and humility help, too. Even in the final chapters of life, a light-hearted comment or a shared smile can release tension and deepen intimacy. Letting go doesn't mean solemnity; it can mean laughter, surprise, or even mischief.

A Life Aligned With Its Ending

Those who master the art of letting go live lighter, love better, and leave more gracefully. Their final days are marked not by frustration or panic, but by calm presence. They have aligned their life with its natural conclusion, and in doing so, they model a quiet courage for others.

Letting go is, in essence, the final practice of longevity: it is not about extending years, but extending the quality and coherence of a life fully lived.

Ageing teaches us many lessons, but the final one is perhaps the most important: the courage to release what we cannot control and embrace what we can.

To let go is to honor the journey, to lighten the burden on ourselves and those we leave behind, and to prepare for a departure marked by dignity, love, and serenity. It is the last, profound act of living well.

Making Peace with Fear

Fear is the shadow of love. The more we love life, the more we fear its end.

Fear of death is universal, but it wears many disguises — anxiety, busyness, denial, the endless search for 'anti-ageing' miracles. Beneath it all lies the same worry: that when the end comes, we won't be ready.

But readiness is rarely about time; it's about trust. The people who die most peacefully are not necessarily the bravest, but the most accepting. They've stopped fighting life's terms and started honouring them.

Fear shrinks when faced directly when shared without shame. Talk about it. Write about it. Laugh at it, even. The more you bring fear into the light, the less it controls you.

Those who make peace with fear aren't fearless — they're simply truthful. They understand that life and death are two halves of the same whole.

The Art of the Final Bow

Every long life has its final act. And yet, few of us pause to consider how we might take our final bow. Most people imagine that endings are abrupt or chaotic — that death is something to fear, avoid, or deny. But the truth is that a life well lived deserves a life well concluded.

The art of the final bow is not dramatic; it's deliberate. It's a small gesture that says, I was here, I lived fully, and now I'm ready to exit the stage. It's the culmination of everything that came before: the lessons learned, the kindness shared, the love given and received. It is a conscious acknowledgment that the story is complete, and that the exit can be graceful, intentional, and dignified.

The best bows are not grand. They're gentle acknowledgements that life has had its seasons, and that the show must go on without us.

Those who bow well are remembered not for how they died, but for how they lived right up until the last line.

A good death is never a defeat — it's a well-timed exit from a life well-loved.

To bow well is to recognise completion. It's to leave behind generosity, humour, and a certain lightness of spirit. Those who bow gracefully aren't remembered for how they died, but for how beautifully they finished.

Some prepare their farewells in quiet ways — a final note of advice to their grandchildren, a favourite meal shared one last time, or a whispered thank-you to the nurses who helped them through. Others simply smile and say, "I'm ready now."

There's a particular kind of wisdom in that readiness — a peace that no longevity expert can teach, because it belongs only to those who have truly lived.

In the end, dying with dignity isn't about control; it's about coherence.

Your final chapter doesn't need to be perfect — it just needs to be yours.

So take your bow, with grace and gratitude. The lights dim, the audience holds its breath — and what remains is love.

Why the Final Bow Matters

The final bow is not for others — it is as much for the one leaving as for those who remain. It is a moment of reflection, a chance to measure life by its meaning rather than its length.

Taking a deliberate bow offers:

- **Closure** — For yourself and those around you.

- **Peace** — Accepting what has been, what cannot be changed, and what remains.

- **Legacy** — A quiet affirmation of who you are and what you leave behind.

Those who master the final bow do so with calm, clarity, and a sense of completion. It is not about dramatics or fanfare; it is about coherence, courage, and presence.

Practical Ways to Prepare Your Bow:

- **Say what needs to be said** — Express gratitude, love, and forgiveness while you still can.

- **Leave messages or letters** — Even small notes provide comfort and guidance to those left behind.

- **Arrange meaningful moments** — A final gathering, a shared ritual, or simply quiet reflection can be profoundly satisfying.

- **Choose your environment** — Surround yourself with things, people, and memories that bring comfort and dignity.

- **Embrace your own style** — The bow can be quiet, playful, humorous, or solemn — whatever feels authentic to you.

The Emotional Gift of the Final Bow

A well-prepared exit offers peace to everyone involved. Family and friends can witness a life concluded intentionally, without confusion or regret. The dying person can leave knowing that their story is complete — and that their presence will be remembered fondly.

The final bow is also a teaching moment, whether consciously intended or not. It demonstrates resilience, grace, and the profound value of planning, acceptance, and love. By exiting thoughtfully, we show those around us that life and death are interconnected chapters of the same story.

Life is not only measured by years or achievements but by how we handle its ending. The art of the final bow reminds us that death need not be abrupt or chaotic. It can be deliberate, dignified, and infused with the same love, humour, and humanity that characterized the life itself.

Every bow, taken consciously, is a testament: I lived fully. I loved deeply. I leave thoughtfully.

Ritual and Remembrance

Humans have always relied on ritual to make sense of the most profound transitions. Birth, marriage, death — these markers give shape to what might otherwise feel chaotic or incomprehensible. At the end of life, ritual becomes a tool for meaning, connection, and peace.

Rituals remind us that we're part of something larger, that our endings belong to a wider rhythm of life.

Ritual doesn't need to be formal, religious, or expensive. It simply needs intention. A deliberate act signals that life is being honoured and transitions are acknowledged. Ritual gives shape to loss. It can soothe the dying, comfort the living, and transform endings from abrupt departures into graceful pauses.

What matters is not ceremony but meaning — a deliberate pause to say, "This mattered. I mattered."

It can be as simple as planting a tree, writing a farewell note, or gathering loved ones to share memories while the person is still here to laugh along.

For those left behind, ritual becomes remembrance. A song, a recipe, a well-thumbed book — these become small altars of continuity, proof that love outlasts breath.

When we ritualise our goodbyes, we transform death from an abrupt stop into a graceful pause — a comma instead of a full stop in the story of being.

The Value of Ritual

Ritual matters because it provides structure in moments of emotional upheaval. When a loved one nears the end, simple rituals can:

- **Ground attention in what matters.**

- **Create shared moments of comfort.**

- **Leave memories that last long after the person is gone.**

Ritual turns absence into presence. It allows us to hold space for grief, gratitude, and reflection — and to experience the final chapter with mindfulness and care.

Practical Ways to Create Meaningful Rituals:

- **Living Wakes** — Invite friends or family to celebrate life while the person is still present. Stories, music, and laughter honour the life in real time.

- **Memory Projects** — Scrapbooks, video diaries, or letters to loved ones can preserve memories and insights for the next generation.

- **Symbolic Acts** — Plant a tree, light a candle, or place a meaningful object somewhere special. Small gestures can carry enormous emotional weight.

- **Shared Quiet** — Sometimes, ritual is as simple as sitting together in silence, holding hands, or listening to a favourite piece of music.

- **Custom Farewells** — Allow each person to leave a message, memory, or token for the person nearing the end. These small contributions can offer immense comfort and connection.

Ritual as Remembrance

Ritual doesn't stop at death. For those left behind, it becomes remembrance. The song that was played, the letters that were written, the tree that was planted — these are living reminders of the person who has gone.

Remembrance rituals help grief transform into gratitude. They allow us to carry forward the essence of a loved one without clinging to loss. By engaging in these acts, we preserve connection, continuity, and legacy.

Ritual and remembrance are acts of care, both for the dying and for those who remain. They provide meaning in the face of the unknown, order in the midst of chaos, and comfort in the quiet moments between life and death.

When we ritualize our goodbyes, we honour not only the life that was lived but also the love that continues — an enduring testament that life, in all its impermanence, mattered deeply.

The Whole of Life — Why Dying Well Is Living Well

Longevity is often thought of as a race against time — a series of goals, achievements, and habits designed to stretch life as far as possible. But in truth, living long is only half the story. How we approach the end of life — with calm, presence, and dignity — completes it. Longevity is not just about adding time, but about making peace with it.

To die well is not to surrender; it is to honour the journey, to embrace the culmination of years spent loving, learning, and living. It is the quiet triumph of a life fully realized, the final chapter written with intention and care.

To live long is to understand that the goal was never immortality — it was meaning.

Those who live and die well share one thing in common: serenity.

They've made peace with the limits of time, and in doing so, they've learned to fill every remaining moment with gratitude.

To die well is to affirm life — to recognise that its beauty was never in its duration, but in its depth.

And when our moment comes, if we can meet it with the same calm curiosity we once met beginnings, then we've mastered the ultimate art: the art of leaving well.

Lessons of a Well-Lived Life

Those who approach the end with grace share common qualities:

- **Presence** — Being fully engaged in the final days, moments, and conversations.

- **Compassion** — Extending love to others while remaining honest about one's own needs.

- **Preparation** — Arranging practical, emotional, and relational matters so that the transition is smooth.

- **Ritual and Remembrance** — Creating small acts of meaning that honour life and sustain memory.

When these elements are combined, a life — long or short — is elevated from mere duration to enduring significance.

The Gift Left Behind

A life concluded thoughtfully benefits not only the person departing but also those who remain. Family, friends, and caregivers are spared unnecessary confusion, guilt, or regret. They inherit a sense of peace, gratitude, and clarity — a living testament to the love, care, and presence of the one who has gone.

A well-lived ending is itself a final act of generosity. It transforms grief into gratitude, absence into memory, and loss into legacy.

A Gentle Reminder

We cannot control how long we live, nor the exact circumstances of our departure. But we can control how we approach the end. We can choose to leave with clarity, kindness, and dignity — with humour where possible, and grace at all times.

It is this final choice — this conscious, thoughtful bow — that completes the story of a life well-lived.

May we live long enough to know that longevity was never the point — only love was.

As we close this work of shared anecdotes, experiences and, perhaps, some nonagenarian wisdom, we remain grateful for every sunrise we've witnessed, every laugh we've shared, and every lesson we've learned. We don't know how much time we have left, but we're still here, still curious, and still learning.

And that, perhaps, is the greatest secret of all - never stop growing, never stop learning, and never stop appreciating the miraculous gift of being alive.

With love and gratitude,

Evita and Lionel Longe

Our Rule for Longevity #19:

Always remember that your life has been unique. Everyone has their own story. You don't need to share it, you don't need approval for the choices you have made. Go easy on yourself. Remind yourself daily that, if you've come this far, your life has been a magnificent one.

Afterword

When we began writing about longevity, we thought it would be a book about staying young.

It isn't.

It's about staying alive — in curiosity, kindness, and spirit — for as long as we're lucky enough to do so.

Evita: What we've learned along the way is that longevity isn't a race against death. It's a relationship with time. And like any good relationship, it deepens when we stop trying to control it.

We cannot stretch our years indefinitely, but we can stretch their meaning. We can live generously, age gracefully, and, when the time comes, leave thoughtfully. That, to us, is the true art of a long life.

Lionel: Writing about ageing and dying has been humbling, and at times surprising. It has shown us that the end of life is not simply a moment to endure — it is a process that can be approached with grace, humour, and intention. It is the final opportunity to reflect the values, relationships, and joy that have shaped a life.

We've seen people who faced their final chapter with quiet courage, clear wishes, and gentle humour. They were neither heroic nor perfect.

They were simply honest — with themselves and with others. And that honesty, above all else, is the essence of dignity.

Longevity isn't really about numbers. It's about depth — the richness, warmth, and awareness that come from having lived long enough to understand what matters. It isn't about adding years to life — it's about finishing well.

By the time we reach old age, we've learned that longevity isn't a race against death; it's a relationship with time. The irony, of course, is that we only learn how to live once we accept that we won't live forever.

We are, in the end, stories. Our bodies wear out, but our gestures linger — in the people we've influenced, the kindnesses we've passed on, the small improvements we've made to our corner of the world.

Those who reach their nineties and beyond often speak not of triumphs, but of contentment. They've made peace with the idea that no one outruns time. The goal isn't to live forever, but to live fully enough that the thought of forever doesn't frighten us.

So perhaps longevity isn't measured in years after all, but in readiness — the readiness to meet whatever comes next with clarity and calm.

If we can live joyfully and die gently, then we have truly mastered the art of longevity. We live long not by denying our mortality, but by understanding it — by realising that the horizon doesn't diminish the journey, it completes it.

We've spent much of this book talking about living well: keeping the mind sharp, the body moving, the heart open. But living well also means knowing how to stop living — not suddenly or fearfully, but with composure, kindness, and dignity. In youth, we chase beginnings. In age, we learn the art of endings.

If there is a single lesson we hope readers will take away, it is this: the way we leave this world matters. Not because it is grand or spectacular, but because it completes the story of who we are. Living fully is only part of the art; leaving thoughtfully is the other.

So live curiously, love generously, and when the final act comes, take your bow with clarity, presence, and care.

And if we can manage that, we've finished well indeed.

Authors' Note

We didn't set out to write a book. We set out to remember how we got this far without falling over.

This began as a few notes on the back of envelopes — reminders to ourselves about what mattered and what turned out not to.

Somewhere along the way, those notes grew into a map of sorts: not the road to longevity, but the route through a life — with all its potholes, detours, and surprisingly scenic stretches.

We're not longevity experts. We've simply lived long enough to recognise nonsense when we hear it. We've had our gullible moments. Between us we've tried every fad at least once — except perhaps cold plunges; we prefer our shocks to be emotional.

If this book has a purpose, it's to remind you that living well isn't complicated. It's about noticing the morning light, forgiving someone before the day ends, and laughing whenever you can get away with it.

And if you find yourself lucky enough to reach your nineties, I recommend three things above all:

- **Keep learning.**

- **Keep moving.**

- **Keep the kettle handy** — because most of life's big conversations still start with, "I'll put the jug on."

So here we are: still curious, still breathing, still amused that people now call us "elders." It sounds terribly official for someone who still loses their glasses daily.

If you've read this far, thank you — truly. You've shared a little piece of our long story.

Now go and put the jug on and make sure yours lasts long enough to tell.

Acknowledgements

No one lives to ninety-something entirely on their own. Even the fiercely independent need a bit of scaffolding — family, friends, neighbors, and the occasional stranger who chases you after you've left your umbrella on the bus.

First, to our families — the ones who've put up with our opinions, our stories, and our tendency to correct the television. You've been our proof that love is the best longevity supplement there is.

To the friends who've walked beside us literally and figuratively, through every change of season — thank you for the laughter, the loyalty, and for not taking our advice too seriously.

To the doctors, nurses, pharmacists, therapists and patient receptionists who've kept us tuned up and roadworthy: your expertise and kindness has added years to our lives – or at least made the existing ones more comfortable.

To the readers and listeners who've made it to the end of this book: bless you for your attention span. If anything we've written helps you laugh, move, eat or forgive a little more easily, then we've done our job.

And to Time itself – that unpredictable companion who's taken so many things but given back perspective in return. You've been a strict teacher, but we suppose that's what makes us respect you so much.

The authors also acknowledge the Traditional Owners of the Country on which we live and work, from the Turrbal, Jinibara, Gubbi Gubbi and Ningy Ningy People of the Meeanjin regions, to the Whadjuk and Ballardong Nyoongar People of the Boorloo regions. We pay our sincere respects to their Elders, past, present and emerging. We recognise their connection to Country and their caring for and maintaining the land, waters and culture for thousands of years.

May their strength and wisdom be with us today and always.

Reviews Invited

The Real Longevity Authority

95-Year-Old Twins' Advice for a Happy, Healthy Life

The authors and publisher thank you for spending your precious time reading this book. We hope you found it inspirational.

Books, like people, travel further by word of mouth. If this one kept you company, or offered something of value, a quiet word from you—a short review via your bookseller's website—helps it continue its journey.

We thank you sincerely.

Bibliography

The Arbor Company. (2024). *Social Dining for Seniors: Cognitive Health Benefits.*

Beresford, J.. (2021, September 10). *95-year-old twins revealed secret behind their longevity: 'no sex and plenty of Guinness'.* The Irish Post.

Cambieri, G. (2024, December 8). *The importance of connections: Ways to live a longer, healthier life.* Harvard T.H. Chan School of Public Health.

Gefen, T., Weintraub, S., Mesulam, M. M., et al. (2025). Distinct neurobiological profiles of SuperAgers: resistance and resilience to Alzheimer's pathology. Alzheimer's & Dementia: The Journal of the Alzheimer's Association. Northwestern University Feinberg School of Medicine.

Ham, S. (2025, January). *Mental Health and Longevity: The Connection.* Friendly Recovery.

Hardt, Oliver – Psychologist, McGill University, Montreal, *Memory Pruning*

Harvard University – T.H. Chan School of Public Health, *Harvard Optimism Study and An active social life may help you live longer.* Staff Writer. (2019, May 14).

High Point Residence. (2025, March 30). *The Benefits of Social Dining for Seniors*.

Holt-Lunstad J.. (2024, September 16). *Social connection as a critical factor for mental and physical health: evidence, trends, challenges, and future implications*. World Psychiatry.

Kearney, K.. (2018). *The Key To Living A Long Life? These 95-Year-Old Twins Have The Answer*. Family Friendly HQ.

Kim, E. J., & Dimsdale, J. E. (2007). The effect of psychosocial stress on sleep: a review of polysomnographic evidence. Behavioral Sleep Medicine, 5(4), 256–278.

Laurence, E.. (2025, April). *The Surprising Impact Emotions Have on Longevity*. Equinox.

Middleton G.. (2022, October 27). *The Health and Well-being Impacts of Community Shared Meal Programs for Older Populations: A Scoping Review*. Innovation in Aging.

Mitchell, T.. (2022, February 01). *The Retirement Process: A Psychological and Emotional Journey*. UW Retiree Relations.

NOVOS Labs. (2023, May 15). *The Mind-Body Connection: How Mental Health Impacts Longevity and Quality of Life*.

Population Reference Bureau. (2024, March 12). *Later Life.Today's Research on Aging 44: More Than a Feeling: How Social Connection Protects Health in Hardt, O.,* Nader, K., & Nadel, L. (2013). Decay happens: the role of active forgetting in memory. Trends in Cognitive Sciences, 17(3), 111–120. https://doi.org/10.1016/j.tics.2013.01.001